MODERN
HOME
ATLAS

MODERN HOME ATLAS

GEORGE PHILIP

LONDON · MELBOURNE · MILWAUKEE

DIRECTOR OF
CARTOGRAPHY:
HAROLD FULLARD, M. Sc.

CARTOGRAPHIC
EDITOR:
B. M. WILLETT, B.A.

CONTENTS

1   General Reference
     The World: Physical   1:150M
2-3   The World: Political   1:80M
4   Europe: Physical   1:20M
5   British Isles   1:4M
6-7   England and Wales   1:2M
8   Scotland   1:2M
9   Ireland   1:2M
10-11   Central Europe   1:5M
12   France   1:5M
13   Spain and Portugal   1:5M
14-15   Italy and the Balkan States   1:5M
16-17   Scandinavia and the Baltic Lands   1:5M
18-19   U.S.S.R.   1:20M
20   Asia   1:50M
21   South-west Asia   1:20M
22   South Asia   1:20M
23   South-east Asia   1:20M
24   Japan   1:10M
     Southern Japan   1:5M
25   China   1:20M
26-27   Australia   1:12M
     Australia: Physical   1:80M
28   New Zealand   1:6M
     New Zealand and Dependencies   1:60M
     Fiji and Tonga, Samoa Islands   1:12M
29   Africa   1:40M
30-31   Northern Africa   1:15M
32-33   Central and Southern Africa   1:15M
34-35   Canada   1:15M
     Alaska   1:30M
36-37   United States   1:12M
     Hawaii   1:10M
38   Mexico   1:12M
     Panama Canal   1:1M
39   West Indies   1:12M
     Bermuda, Leeward Is., Windward Is.,
     Jamaica and Trinidad and Tobago   1:8M
40-41   South America – North   1:16M
42   South America – South   1:16M
44-47   Index

Illustrations

Cover: *rain forest in Sumatra;* **half-title:** *evening light on Thamserku, Nepal;* **title:** *Bryce Canyon, Utah, U.S.A.;* **contents:** *Tahiti with the island of Moorea in the distance. All illustrations supplied by Bruce Coleman Ltd.*

British Library Cataloguing in Publication Data

Modern home atlas – 5th ed.
   1. Atlases, British
   912   G1021

ISBN 0 540 05390 2

© 1981 George Philip and Son Limited, London

GENERAL REFERENCE

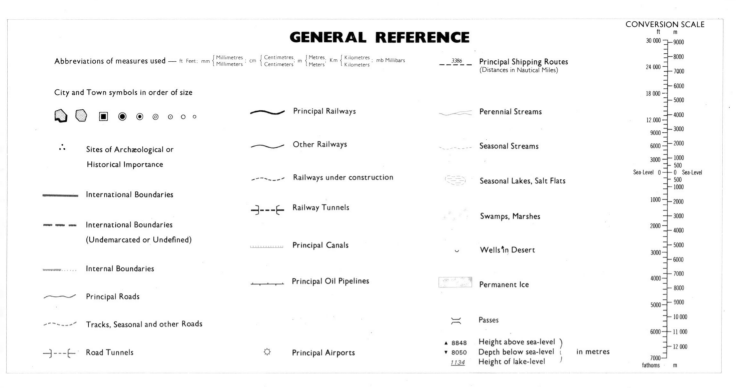

THE WORLD
Physical
1:150 000 000

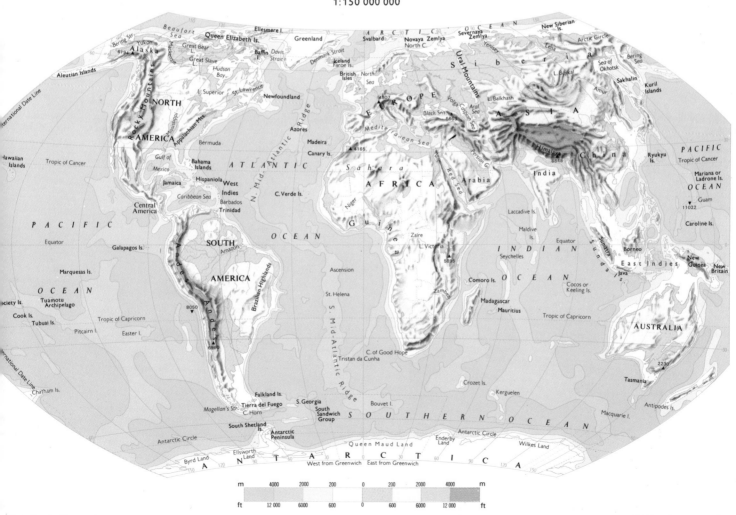

Projection: Hammer Equal Area

COPYRIGHT. GEORGE PHILIP & SON. LTD.

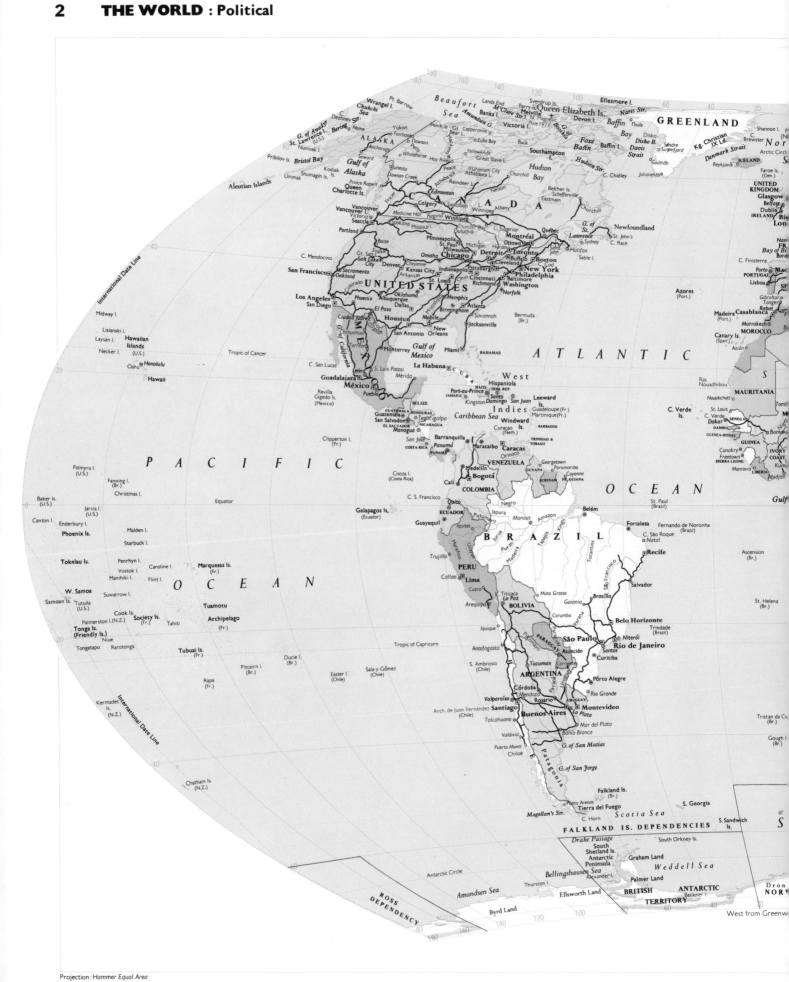

Projection: Hammer Equal.Area

1 : 20 000 000

| 100 | 0 | 100 | 200 | 300 | 400 | 500 miles |
| 100 | 0 | 200 | 400 | 600 | 800 km |

COPYRIGHT. GEORGE PHILIP & SON, LTD.

Ob
Ural
CASPIAN SEA −28

Ural Mountains
Obshchsyrt
Kama
Pechora
Narodnaya 1617

Tundra
Volga Uplands
Volga
Don
Kuban
Terek
Rion
Kura
Araks
Caucasus 5633
Elbruz 5633
Kazbek 5186

L. Urmia
Kurdistan
Armenia
Anatolia
Euphrates

White Sea
Kanin Peninsula
Kola Peninsula
Mezen
N. Dvina
Onega
L. Onega
Svir
Ladoga
Rybinsk Res.
Volga
Oka
Don
Manych
Tsimlyansk Res.
Sea of Azov
Str. of Kerch
Crimea

Central Russian Uplands
Ukraine
Dniepr (Dnieper)
Bug
Danube
BLACK SEA 2211
Bosporus
S. of Marmara
Vidd 1766
Aegean Sea

Finland
Lapland
Kjölen
Gol. of Bothnia
Scandinavia
Nordknn
North Cape

Pripyat Marshes
Pripyat (Pripet)
European Plain
Dnestr (Dniester)
Prut
Niemen
Wista (Vistula)
Odra (Odder)

Carpathians
Transylvanian Alps
Plain of Hungary 2655
Wallachia
Balkans
Peninsula
Danube
Morava
Tisza
Drava
Sava
Moldau
Balkan Peninsula
Pindus
Morea
5121 C. Matapan
Crete

Gotland
Gulf of Finland
Neva
L. Chudskoye
W. Dvina
G. of Riga
BALTIC SEA
North Sea

Vesterålen
Lofoten
2123 Kebnekaise
Torne
Ume
Indals
Milaren
Vänern
Vättern

Galdhøpiggen 2469
Kattegat
Skagerrak
Jutland
Elbe
Weser

Dinaric Alps
ADRIATIC SEA
Str. of Otranto
Ionian Is.
Ionian Sea
Calabria
Etna 3263
Sicily
Str. of Messina

Apennines
Gran Sasso 2914
Vesuvius 1277
Tyrrhenian Sea
Tiber
Str. of Bonifacio

NORWEGIAN SEA
3734

Harz 1142
Ez Geb
Bohemian For.
Sudetes
Black For.
Vosges
Jura
Alps
Mt. Blanc 4807
Taunus
Rhine
Westerwald

FISHER
VIKING
Lindesnes
FORTIES
GERMAN BIGHT
Helgoland
NORTH SEA
DOGGER
Dogger Bank
HUMBER
Netherlands
THAMES

Ligurian Sea
Corsica
Sardinia
C. Blanco
Po
Rhone
G. of Lions

Arctic Circle
SOUTH EAST ICELAND
Myrdals Jokull 2119
Iceland 1491
Fisher Bank

Faroe Is.
FAEROES
Shetland Is.
FAIR ISLE
Orkney Is.
CROMARTY
FORTH
TYNE
DOVER

Central Massif 1886
Cevennes
Ardennes
Meuse
Seine
Garonne
Rhone

MEDITERRANEAN SEA
Maritime Atlas
Plateau of the Shotts

HEBRIDES
Ben Nevis 1343
Great Britain
Snowdon 1085
Irish Sea
British Isles
Ireland
Thames
English Channel
PORTLAND
WIGHT
PLYMOUTH
Brittany
Loire

BAILEY
ROCKALL
Rockall
Hebrides
FASTNET
LUNDY
SOLE
Valentia I.
SHANNON
C. Clear
Land's End

Bay of Biscay 4861
FINISTERRE
C. Finisterre
Douro
Tejo (Tagos)

Pyrenees 3404
Old Castile
New Castile
Iberian Peninsula
Sierra de Guadarrama
Cantabrian Mts.
Pico de Aneto
Guadalquivir
Sierra Morena
Sierra Nevada 3478
Andalusia
C. Trafalgar
Str. of Gibraltar
C. Spartel
Er. Rif
Guadiana
C. St. Vincent

ATLANTIC OCEAN

Projection Bonne
West from Greenwich 0 East from Greenwich
ROCKALL Sea areas are named in capitals

Cyprus 1951

ft		m
12 000	4000	
6000	2000	
3000	1000	
1200	400	
600	200	
0	0	
	−200	−600
2000	6000	
4000	12 000	
m		ft

1:4 000 000

The DISTRICTS of Northern Ireland have been numbered and can be identified by reference to this table.

1	Londonderry	14	Craigavon
2	Limavady	15	Armagh
3	Coleraine	16	Newry & Mourne
4	Ballymoney	17	Banbridge
5	Moyle	18	Down
6	Larne	19	Lisburn
7	Ballymena	20	Antrim
8	Magherafelt	21	Newtownabbey
9	Cookstown	22	Carrickfergus
10	Strabane	23	North Down
11	Omagh	24	Ards
12	Fermanagh	25	Castlereagh
13	Dungannon	26	Belfast

1 Merseyside
2 Greater Manchester
3 West Yorkshire
4 South Yorkshire
5 West Glamorgan
6 Mid Glamorgan
7 South Glamorgan

Projection: Conical with two standard parallels

West from Greenwich   East from Greenwich
COPYRIGHT. GEORGE PHILIP & SON. LTD.

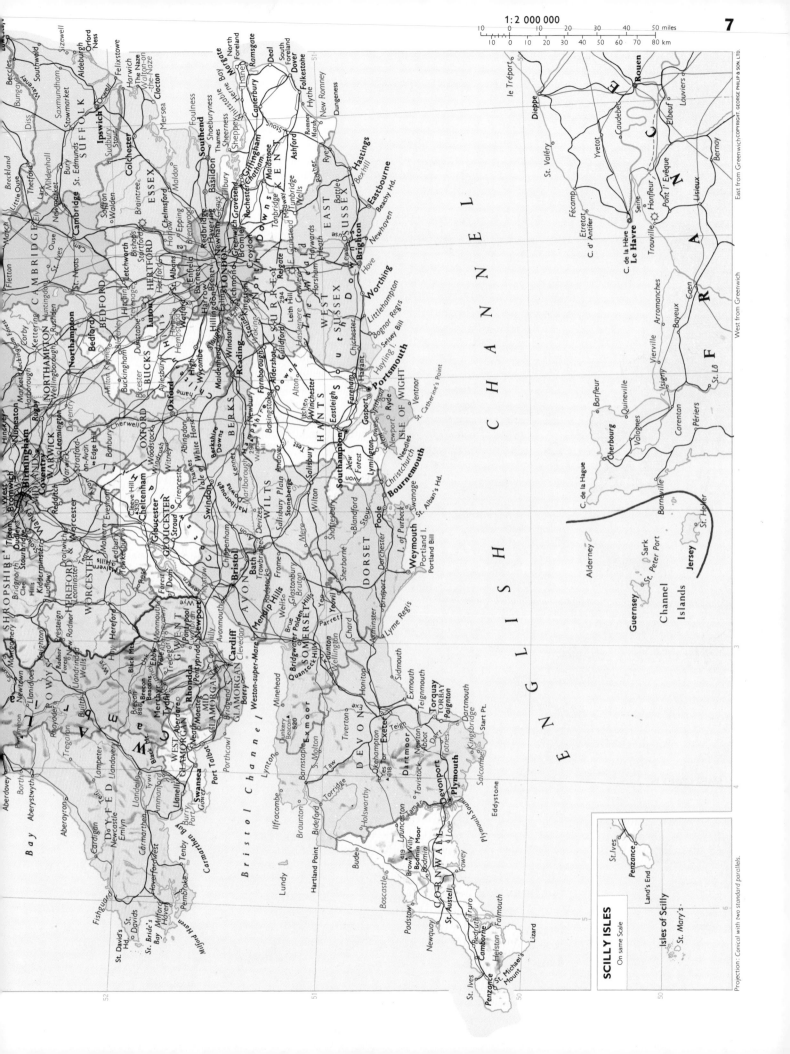

1:2 000 000

10   0   10   20   30   40   50 miles

10   0   10   20   30   40   50   60   70   80 km

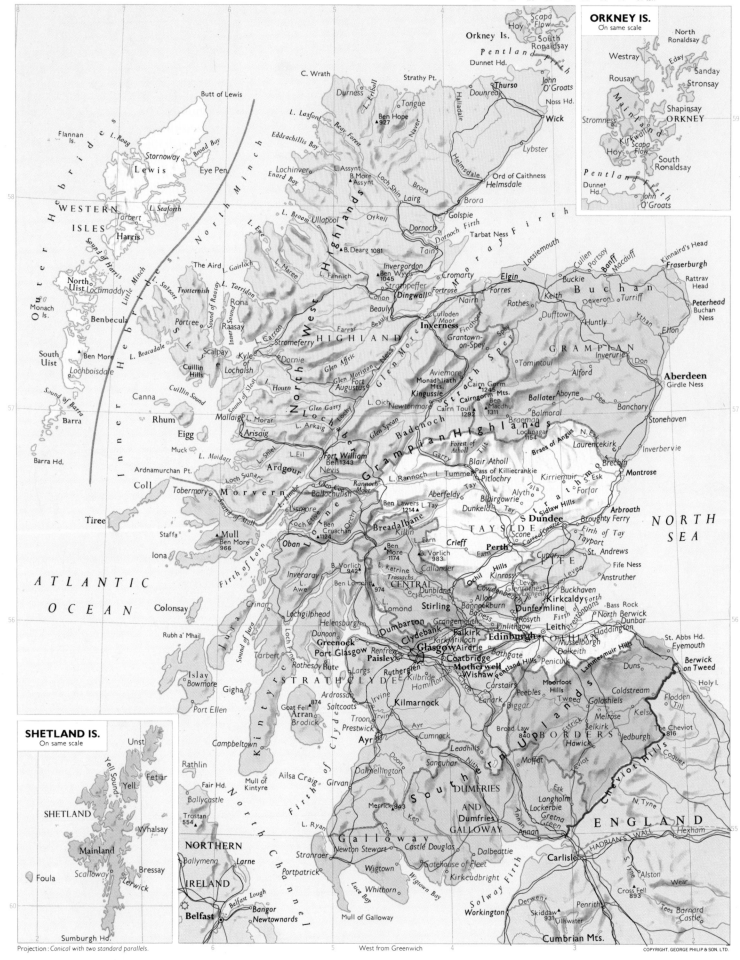

ORKNEY IS.
On same scale

ORKNEY

SHETLAND IS.
On same scale

SHETLAND

Projection : Conical with two standard parallels.

West from Greenwich

COPYRIGHT. GEORGE PHILIP & SON, LTD.

1 : 2 000 000

Projection: Conical with two standard parallels.

West from Greenwich

COPYRIGHT. GEORGE PHILIP & SON. LTD.

Towns underlined in Northern Ireland give their names to the Districts in which they stand

The remaining Districts are:—

1	Fermanagh	5	Castlereagh
2	Moyle	6	Ards
3	Newtownabbey	7	Down
4	North Down	8	Newry & Mourne

NORTH SEA

BALTIC

NETHERLANDS
's-Gravenhage (The Hague)
Hoek van Holland
Amsterdam
Haarlem
Leiden
Rotterdam
Utrecht
Apeldoorn
Enschede
Dordrecht
Breda
Leeuwarden
Groningen
Assen
Meppel
Zwolle
Deventer
Nijmegen
Arnhem
Den Helder
Alkmaar
Hoorn
Kampen
Sneek
Texel
Terschelling
Ameland
Schiermonnikoog
IJsselmeer

Vlissingen
Zeebrugge
Oostende
Brugge (Gand)
Antwerpen
Gent
Aalst
Mechelen
Brussel (Bruxelles)
Leuven
Maastricht
Liège
Namur
Charleroi
BELGIUM
FLANDRE
Kortrijk
Lille
Roubaix
Tourcoing
Tournai
Mons
Douai
Valenciennes
Cambrai

LUX.
Luxembourg
Trier
Longwy
Thionville
Metz
SAARLAND
Saarbrücken
Kaiserslautern
Neunkirchen
LORRAINE
Nancy
Toul
Lunéville
Épinal
St. Dié
Colmar
Mulhouse
Belfort
Montbéliard

FRANCE
St. Quentin
Laon
Soissons
Reims
Châlons-sur-Marne
Épernay
Château-Thierry
Vitry-le-François
Bar-le-Duc
Verdun
Troyes
Aube
Chaumont
Langres
Plateau de Langres
Dijon
Besançon
Dôle
Beaune
Autun
Le Creusot
Mâcon
Bourg
Lyon
Villeurbanne
St. Étienne
Vienne
Chambéry
Grenoble
DAUPHINÉ
PROVENCE
Nîmes
Avignon
Arles
Aix
Marseille
Cannes
Nice
MONACO
Menton

NIEDERSACHSEN
Flensburg
Schleswig
Kiel
HOLSTEIN
Rendsburg
Neumünster
Lübeck
Hamburg
Altona
Harburg
Lüneburg
Bremerhaven
Bremen
Oldenburg
Wilhelmshaven
Emden
Cuxhaven
Helgoland
Ost-friesische Inseln
Deutsche Bucht
Wangerooge
Borkum
Norderney
Osnabrück
Münster
Hannover
Braunschweig
Hildesheim
Herford
Bielefeld
Detmold
Paderborn
Kassel
NORDRHEIN-WESTFALEN
Duisburg
Essen
Dortmund
Gelsenkirchen
Bochum
Hagen
Wuppertal
Remscheid
Düsseldorf
Mönchengladbach
Krefeld
Köln (Cologne)
Bonn
Aachen
Eupen
Koblenz
RHEINLAND
Westerwald
Taunus
WEST GERMANY
Wiesbaden
Mainz
Frankfurt
Offenbach
Hanau
Darmstadt
Worms
PFALZ
Ludwigshafen
Mannheim
Heidelberg
Speyer
Karlsruhe
Pforzheim
BADEN
Baden
Freiburg
Strasbourg
Heilbronn
Stuttgart
Ludwigsburg
Esslingen
WÜRTTEMBERG
Tübingen
Reutlingen
Ulm
Schwäbische Alb
Rottweil
Schwarzwald
Donau (Danube)
Tuttlingen
Konstanz
Friedrichshafen

Göttingen
Nordhausen
Brocken 1142
Halberstadt
Magdeburg
Dessau
Wittenberg
Bernburg
EAST GERMANY
Halle
Leipzig
Merseburg
Naumburg
Erfurt
Weimar
Jena
Gera
Zeitz
Gotha
Meiningen
Thüringer Wald
Schweinfurt
Würzburg
Bamberg
Erlangen
Fürth
Nürnberg
Ansbach
Amberg
Regensburg
BAYERN
Ingolstadt
Donauwörth
Augsburg
Landshut
München (Munich)
Freising
Rosenheim
Memmingen
Kempten

Berlin
Charlottenburg
Potsdam
Spandau
Brandenburg
Luckenwalde
Cottbus
Forst
Dresden
Meissen
Bautzen
Görlitz
Karl-Marx-Stadt (Chemnitz)
Zwickau
Glauchau
Reichenbach
Plauen
Hof
Bayreuth
Erzgebirge
Cheb
Karlovy Vary
Chomutov
Most
Teplice
Ústí nad Labem
Litoměřice
Mladá Boleslav
Hradec Králové
Pardubice
Praha (Prague)
Kladno
Beroun
Plzeň (Pilsen)
Pribram
CZECHOSLOVAKIA
České Budějovice
Tábor
Jihlava
Brno (Brünn)
Znojmo

Rostock
Wismar
Schwerin
Güstrow
Neubrandenburg
Stralsund
Rügen
Sassnitz
Greifswald
Usedom
Świnoujście
Wolin
Szczecin (Stettin)
Oder Haff
Goleniów
Stargard
Koszalin
Kołobrzeg
Piła
POLAND
Gorzów
Zielona Góra
Głogów
Legnica
Wrocław
Wałbrzych
Jelenia Góra
Riesengebirge
Śnieżka
Sudety

AUSTRIA
ÖSTERREICH
Linz
Wels
Steyr
Melk
St. Pölten
Wien (Vienna)
Baden
Wiener Neustadt
Salzburg
Bad Ischl
Gmunden
Innsbruck
Kufstein
SALZBURG
TIROL
Gross Glockner 3797
Brenner 1371
KÄRNTEN
Klagenfurt
Villach
Lienz
STEIERMARK
Graz
Leoben
Bruck
Semmering
BURGENLAND

SWITZERLAND
SCHWEIZ
Basel
Winterthur
Zürich
Zug
Luzern
St. Gallen
Aarau
Solothurn
Bern
Biel
Neuchâtel
La Chaux-de-Fonds
Lausanne
Genève
Montreux
Interlaken
Thun
Chur
Davos
St. Moritz
Engadin
LIECHTENSTEIN
Feldkirch
VORARLBERG
Arlberg
Mt. Blanc 4807
Matterhorn 4478
Mte. Rosa 4634
Gotthard
Splügenpass
Simplonpass
Domodossola
Locarno
Bellinzona
Lugano
Lago Maggiore

ITALY
ITALIA
Bolzano
Bressanone
Merano
Ortles 3899
Adamello 3554
TRENTINO
ALTO-ADIGE
Trento
Rovereto
FRIULI-VENEZIA-GIULIA
Udine
Gorizia
Trieste
Valtellina
L. di Como
Como
Bergamo
Brescia
Lago di Garda
LOMBARDIA
Milano (Milan)
Novara
Pavia
Cremona
Mantova (Mantua)
Verona
Vicenza
Padova (Padua)
VENETO
Treviso
Vittorio Veneto
Venezia (Venice)
Golfo di Venezia
Chioggia
Rovigo
Adige
Ferrara
PIEMONTE
Torino
Chivasso
Casale
Vercelli
Asti
Alessandria
Cuneo
Mondovì
Pinerolo
Saluzzo
Mt. Viso 3841
Col di Tenda
EMILIA-ROMAGNA
Piacenza
Parma
Reggio
Modena
Bologna
Imola
Faenza
Forlì
Cesena
Rímini
Pésaro
Ravenna
LIGURIA
Savona
Genova (Genoa)
Golfo di Génova
La Spézia
Carrara
Massa
San Marino
Pistoia
Prato
Firenze (Florence)
Lucca
Pisa

ADRIATIC SEA
Ljubljana
Zagreb
Maribor
Celje
Rijeka
Istra
Koper
HRVATSKA
Karlovac
Sisak
Krk
Cres
Lošinj
Dugi Otok
Zadar
Pag

1 : 5 000 000

50   0   50   100 miles
50   0   50   100   150 km

Countries / Regions

R.S.F.S.R.
LITHUANIAN S.S.R.
BYELORUSSIAN S.S.R.
P O L A N D
U.K R A I N I A N S.S.R.
U. S. S. R.
MOLDAVIAN S.S.R.
S L O V A K I A
H U N G A R Y
R U M A N I A
Transilvania
Carpații Meridionali
Valahia
Banat
BULGARIA
GOSLAVIA (YUGOSLAVIA)
BLACK SEA
Zatoka Gdańska
Pojezierze Mazurskie

Cities and towns

Wejherowo, Sopot, Gdynia, Gdańsk (Danzig), Elbląg, Malbork, Kwidzyń, Braniewo, Kaliningrad (Königsberg), Pregel, Chernyakhovsk, Gusev, Zelenogradsk, Starogard, Grudziądz, Chełmno, Tczew, Ostróda, Olsztyn, Kętrzyn, Giżycko, 309, Suwałki, Augustów, Vilnius, Alitus, Varena, Lida, Molodechno, Borisov, Gorki, Minsk, Mogilev, Krichev

Iława, Mława, Lipno, Włocławek, Wabrzeżno, Rypin, Toruń, Inowrocław, Gniezno, Września, Notec, Bydgoszcz, Chełmża, Ciechanów, Ostrołęka, Ostrów Mazowiecka, Brańsk, Hajnówka, Łomża, Białystok, 238, Sokółka, Grodno, Neman, Mosty, Volkovysk, Slonim, Skchara, Baranovichi, Bobruysk, Gomel, Berezina

Pułtusk, Wkra, Płock, Łowicz, Pruszków, Warszawa (Warsaw), Mińsk Mazowiecki, Siedlce, Biała Podlaska, Brest, Zhabinka, Bereza, Luninets, Pripyat, Kalinkovichi, Ptich, Drut, Sozh

Koło, Kutno, Łęczyca, Żyrardów, Grójec, Otwock, Łuków, Międzyrzec Podlaski, Włodawa, Czeremcha, Kalisz, Zduńska Wola, Łódź, Skierniewice, Pilica, Dubrovitsa, Sarny, 316, Uzh, Desna

Ostrów Wielkopolski, Turek, Konin, Piotrków Trybunalski, Tomaszów Mazowiecki, Radom, Kozienice, Puławy, Lublin, Chełm, Kovel, Styr, Gorin, Sluch, Korosten, Radomyshl, Kiev, Borispol

Opole, Częstochowa, Kielce, Ostrowiec Świętokrzyski, Skarżysko, Kraśnik, Zamość, Vladimir Volynskiy, Lutsk, Rovno, Ostrog, Shepetovka, Zhitomir, Berdichev, Kazatin, Belaya Tserkov

Zabrze, Gliwice, Bytom, Sosnowiec, Chorzów, Katowice, Kraków, Wieliczka, Tarnów, Wisła (Vistula), Dąbrowa, Tarnobrzeg, Przeworsk, 390, San, Sandomierz, Kamenka Bugskaya, Radekhov, Brody, Kremenets, Starokonstantinov, Zhmerinka, Vinnitsa, Uman, 384, Bug, Pervomaisk

Racibórz, Bielsko-Biała, Nowy Sącz, Jasło, Krosno, Dukelský Pr. 502, Sanok, Przemyśl, Gorodok, Lvov, 471, Sambor, Dnestr, Drogobych, Borislav, Stryi, Turka, Ternopol, Zolochev, Buchach, Chortkov, Zaleshchiki, Khmelnitskiy, Kamenets-Podolskiy, Mogilev-Podolskiy, Soroki, Beltsy

Ostrava, Frýdek-Místek, Český Těšín, Jablunkovský Prů, Západné Beskydy, Tatry, Východné Beskydy, 1725, 2655, Žilina, Ružomberok, Nízke Tatry, Prešov, Košice, Uzhgorod, Mukachevo, 931, Beregovo, Khust, Sighet, Ivano-Frankovsk, Nadvornaya 1881, Yablonitse, Kolomyya, Snyatin, Chernovtsy, Storozhinets, Yedintsy, Khotin, Dorohoi, Botoșani, Dnestr, Kotovsk, Moldavian

Kremnica, Nitra, N. Zámky, Komárno, Slovenské Rudohorie, Banská Bystrica, Zvolen, Banská Štiavnica, Lučenec, Sátoraljaújhely, Hron, Sajó, Bodrog, Tokaj, Miskolc, Eger, Mezőkövesd, Nyíregyháza, Hajdúböszörmény, Satu Mare, Carei, Baia Mare, Pietrosul 2305, Sighet, Radauti, Suceava, Vatra-Dornei, Iași, Kishinev, 429, Bendery, Tiraspol

Győr, Tatabánya, Esztergom, Vác, Gyöngyös, Hatvan, Jászberény, Újpest, Budapest, Szolnok, Karcag, Debrecen, Dej, Someș, Bistrița 2102, Pietrosul, Piatra Neamț, Roman, Bacău, Vaslui, Bîrlad, Bacău, Odessa, Belgorod-Dnestrovskiy, Ozero Sasyk

Székesfehérvár, Cegléd, Nagykőrös, Mezőtúr, Oradea, Salonta, Cluj, Turda, Tîrgu Mureș, Praid, Odorhei, Miercurea Ciuc, Bretcu, Focșani, Tecuci, Bolgrad, Reni, Ismail, Kiliya

Veszprém, Dunaújváros, Kecskemét, Kiskunfélegyháza, Békéscsaba, Mții Bihor 1848, Abrud, Aiud, Alba-Iulia, Medias, Sighișoara, Sibiu, Făgăraș, Sfântu Gheorghe, Brașov, Pîrîul Sarat, Galați, Brăila, 467, Tulcea, Sulina

Kaposvár, Balaton, Dunaföldvár, Kalocsa, Kiskőrös, Kiskunhalas, Szentes, Hódmezővásárhely, Makó, Szeged, Arad, Lugoj, Deva, Hunedoara, Simeria, Brad, Mureș, Negru, Crișul Alb, Turnu Roșu, Vf. Negoiu 2535, Omul 2507, Cîmpulung, Buzău, Dunărea (Danube), Călărași

Pécs, Mohács, Szekszárd, Batászek, Baja, Subotica, Timișoara, Caransebeș, Petroșeni 350, Paringul-Mare 2518, 2509, Peleaga, Târgu-Jiu, Rîmnicu Vîlcea, Pitești, Tîrgoviște, Ploiești, Ialomița, Cernavodă, Constanța, Mangalia, Tolbukhin

Osijek, Vinkovci, Sombor, Novi Sad, Petrovaradin, Sremska Mitrovica, Zemun, Pančevo, Vršac, Bela Crkva, Resița, Porta Orientalis, Mehadia, Portile de Fier, Orsova, Turnu-Severin, Jiu, Olt, Slatina, Argeș, București (Bucharest), Dâmbovița, Oltenița, Giurgiu, Ruse (Ruschuk), Silistra

Brod, Bosna, Brčko, Bijeljina, Tuzla, Zenica, Zvornik, Han Pijesak, 1346, Sarajevo, Titova Užice, Valjevo, Smederevo, Požarevac, Beograd (Belgrade), Sava, Morava, Bor, Negotin, Timok, Zaječar, Čačak, Kragujevac, Vidin, Lom, Craiova, Caracal, Corabia, Turnu Măgurele, Zimnicea, Vedea

1:5 000 000

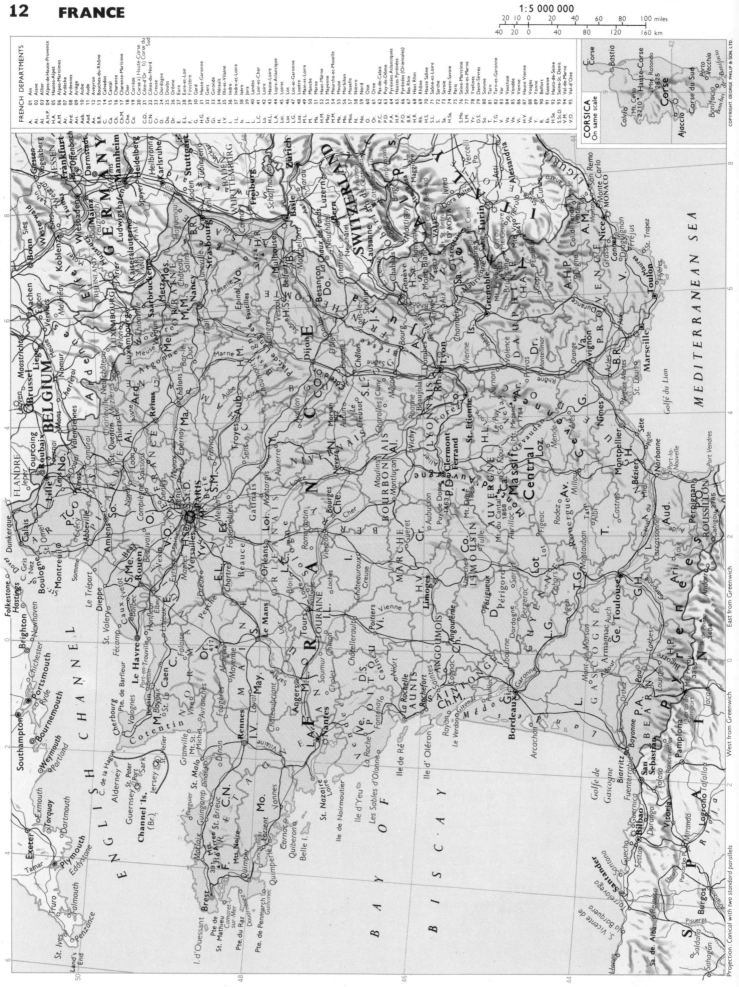

FRENCH DEPARTMENTS

A.	Ain	01
Ai.	Aisne	02
Al.	Allier	03
A.H.P.	Alpes-de-Haute-Provence	04
H.A.	Hautes-Alpes	05
A.M.	Alpes-Maritimes	06
Ard.	Ardèche	07
Ard.	Ardennes	08
Ari.	Ariège	09
Au.	Aube	10
Aud.	Aude	11
Av.	Aveyron	12
B.R.	Bouches-du-Rhône	13
C.	Calvados	14
Ca.	Cantal	15
Ch.M.	Charente-Maritime	17
Che.	Cher	18
C.	Corrèze	19
C.O.	Côte-d'Or	21
C.N.	Côtes-du-Nord	22
Cr.	Creuse	23
D.	Dordogne	24
Do.	Doubs	25
Dr.	Drôme	26
E.	Eure	27
E.L.	Eure-et-Loir	28
F.	Finistère	29
G.	Gard	30
H.G.	Haute-Garonne	31
Ge.	Gers	32
Gi.	Gironde	33
H.	Hérault	34
I.V.	Ille-et-Vilaine	35
I.	Indre	36
I.L.	Indre-et-Loire	37
Is.	Isère	38
J.	Jura	39
L.	Landes	40
L.C.	Loir-et-Cher	41
Lo.	Loire	42
H.L.	Haute-Loire	43
L.A.	Loire-Atlantique	44
Loi.	Loiret	45
Lot	Lot	46
L.G.	Lot-et-Garonne	47
Loz.	Lozère	48
M.L.	Maine-et-Loire	49
Ma.	Manche	50
M.	Marne	51
H.M.	Haute-Marne	52
May.	Mayenne	53
M.M.	Meurthe-et-Moselle	54
Meu.	Meuse	55
Mo.	Morbihan	56
Mos.	Moselle	57
N.	Nièvre	58
No.	Nord	59
O.	Oise	60
Or.	Orne	61
P.C.	Pas-de-Calais	62
P.D.	Puy-de-Dôme	63
P.A.	Pyrénées-Atlantiques	64
H.P.	Hautes-Pyrénées	65
P.O.	Pyrénées (Orientales)	66
B.R.	Bas Rhin	67
H.R.	Haut Rhin	68
Rh.	Rhône	69
H.S.	Haute-Saône	70
S.L.	Saône-et-Loire	71
Sa.	Sarthe	72
Sav.	Savoie	73
H.Sa.	Haute-Savoie	74
	Paris	75
S.Me.	Seine-Maritime	76
S.M.	Seine-et-Marne	77
Y.	Yvelines	78
D.S.	Deux-Sèvres	79
So.	Somme	80
T.	Tarn	81
T.G.	Tarn-et-Garonne	82
Va.	Var	83
V.	Vaucluse	84
Ve.	Vendée	85
Vi.	Vienne	86
H.V.	Haute Vienne	87
Vo.	Vosges	88
Y.	Yonne	89
B.	Belfort	90
E.	Essonne	91
H.Se.	Hauts-de-Seine	92
S.S.D.	Seine-St-Denis	93
V.	Val-de-Marne	94
V.O.	Val-d'Oise	95

Corsica

C.O. Corse (a) Haute-Corse 2B
C.S. Corse (b) Corse du Sud 2A

CORSICA
On same scale

Projection: Conical with two standard parallels

1:5 000 000

50   50   0   50   100 miles
50   0   50   100   150 km

F R A N C E

Montpellier   Béziers   Narbonne   Golfe du Lion   Perpignan   Port Vendres

Toulouse   Carcassonne   Foix   Pau   Lourdes   Tarbes

Bayonne   Biarritz   Hendaye   San Sebastián

Bay of Biscay

P y r é n é e s   ANDORRA

Gerona   **Barcelona**   Badalona   Sabadell   Tarrasa   Hospitalet   Sitges

C A T A L U Ñ A   Tarragona   Lérida   Huesca

Zaragoza   A R A G O N   Tudela   Calatayud

NAVARRA   Pamplona   Logroño   LA RIOJA   Soria

Bilbao   Vitoria   VASCONGADAS   Miranda   Burgos

B A L E A R E S   Menorca   Mallorca   **Palma**   Cabrera

Ibiza   Formentera   S. Antonio

Castellón de la Plana   **Valencia**   Albufera de Valencia   Golfo de Valencia   Sagunto   Villarreal

Teruel   Sa. de Albarracín   Cuenca   Serranía de Cuenca

Gandía   Denia   C. Nao   Benidorm   **Alicante**   Elche   Orihuela

Murcia   Lorca   Cartagena   Mar Menor   C. de Palos

Albacete   La Roda   Almansa   Yecla

S P A I N

MADRID   El Escorial   Alcalá de Henares   Guadalajara   Aranjuez

Segovia   Ávila   Sierra de Gredos   Toledo   Montes de Toledo

CASTILLA LA VIEJA   CASTILLA LA NUEVA   L A M A N C H A

Valladolid   Palencia   Medina   Arévalo   Salamanca   Zamora

León   Sierra de la Demanda   Astorga

Oviedo   Gijón   Mieres   ASTURIAS   Cordillera Cantábrica

Santander   Picos de Europa   Reinosa

Ciudad Real   Valdepeñas   Manzanares   Tomelloso   Alcázar de San Juan

Linares   Jaén   Úbeda   Baeza   Andújar

S i e r r a   M o r e n a

Córdoba   Montilla   Lucena   Puente Genil

Granada   Sa. Nevada   Mulhacén 3478   Guadix   Loja

Málaga   Vélez Málaga   Marbella   Torremolinos   Estepona

Almería   C. de Gata   Adra   Motril

Sevilla   Utrera   Carmona   Écija   Osuna   Morón

E X T R E M A D U R A   Cáceres   Badajoz   Mérida   Trujillo   Plasencia

Talavera de la Reina   Navalmoral

P O R T U G A L

Lisboa   Setúbal   Sintra   Estoril

Porto   Coimbra   Aveiro   Ovar

BEIRA ALTA   BEIRA BAIXA   BEIRA LITORAL

TRAS OS MONTES   ALTO DOURO   MINHO   DOURO LITORAL

Braga   Viana do Castelo   Lamego   Viseu   Guarda   Covilhã

ESTREMADURA   RIBATEJO   Santarém   Tomar

ALTO ALENTEJO   BAIXO ALENTEJO   Évora   Beja

A L G A R V E   Faro   Loulé   C. de S. Vicente   Sagres

G A L I C I A   La Coruña   Santiago de Compostela   Vigo   Pontevedra   Orense   Lugo

C. Ortegal   C. Finisterre   El Ferrol   Ribadeo

A T L A N T I C   O C E A N

Huelva   Golfo de Cádiz   **Cádiz**   Jerez   Sanlúcar de Barrameda   Puerto de Sta. María   San Fernando   Chiclana

C. Trafalgar   Tarifa   Strait of Gibraltar   Gibraltar (Br.)   La Línea de la Concepción   Pt. Europa

Ceuta (Sp.)   Tetouan   Tanger   M O R O C C O

A L G E R I A   Alger   Blida   Boufarik   Koléa   Khemis Miliana   El Asnam   Oran   Mostaganem   C. Falcon   C. Caxine

M E D I T E R R A N E A N   S E A

East from Greenwich   West from Greenwich

Projection: Conical with two standard parallels

ICELAND
on the same scale
as general map

1:5 000 000

20 10 0 20 40 60 80 100 miles
40 20 0 40 80 120 160 km

East from Greenwich

Projection: Conical with two standard parallels

	R.S.F.S.R.
1.	Daghestan A.S.S.R.
2.	Kabardino–Balkar A.S.S.R.
3.	Mari A.S.S.R.
4.	Mordovian A.S.S.R.
5.	North Ossetian A.S.S.R.
6.	Tatar A.S.S.R.
7.	Udmurt A.S.S.R.
8.	Chuvash A.S.S.R.
9.	Checheno–Ingush A.S.S.R.
	AZERBAIJAN
10.	Nakhichevan A.S.S.R.
	GEORGIA
11.	Abkhaz A.S.S.R.
12.	Adzhar A.S.S.R.

Projection: Conical Orthomorphic with two standard parallels

East from Greenwich

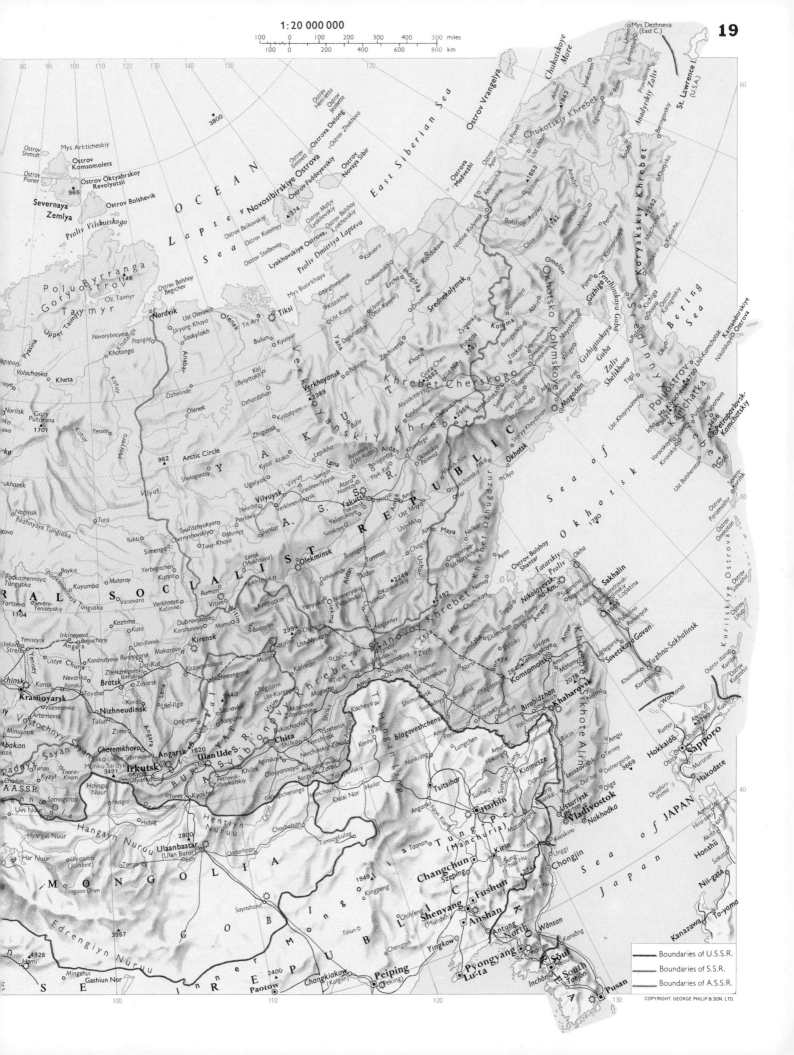

1:50 000 000

200 0 200 400 600 800 1000 miles
200 0 400 800 1200 1600 km

COPYRIGHT. GEORGE PHILIP & SON. LTD.

Projection: Bonne

East from Greenwich

Oceans and Seas
PACIFIC OCEAN
ARCTIC OCEAN
INDIAN OCEAN
Bering Sea
Sea of Okhotsk
Sea of Japan
East China Sea
Yellow Sea
South China Sea
Bay of Bengal
Arabian Sea
Red Sea
Black Sea
Caspian Sea
Mediterranean Sea
Laptev Sea
Kara Sea
Barents Sea
Baltic Sea
North Sea
Celebes Sea
Sulu Sea
Banda Sea
Seram Sea
Flores Sea
Java Sea
Persian Gulf
G. of Oman
G. of Aden
Tropic of Cancer
Arctic Circle
Equator

Countries and Regions
U. S. S. R.
CHINESE REPUBLIC
MONGOLIA
INNER MONGOLIA
MANCHURIA
SINKIANG UIGUR
TIBET
INDIA
PAKISTAN
AFGHANISTAN
IRAN (PERSIA)
IRAQ
SAUDI ARABIA
NEPAL
BANGLADESH
BURMA
THAILAND (SIAM)
VIETNAM
LAOS
CAMBODIA
MALAYSIA
PENINSULAR MALAYSIA
INDONESIA
PHILIPPINES
SRI LANKA (CEYLON)
KASHMIR
BHUTAN
OMAN
UNITED ARAB EMIRATES
QATAR
BAHRAIN
KUWAIT
YEMEN
SOUTH YEMEN
SYRIA
LEBANON
ISRAEL
JORDAN
TURKEY
CYPRUS
EGYPT
LIBYA
SUDAN
ETHIOPIA
SOMALI REP.
KENYA
UGANDA
TANZANIA
RWANDA
BURUNDI
ZAIRE
ZAMBIA
MALAWI
EUROPE
UNITED KINGDOM
ICELAND
AFRICA
AUSTRALIA
New Guinea
Irian Jaya
BRUNEI

Cities and Towns
London, Paris, Roma, Berlin, Warszawa, Wien, Beograd, Thessaloniki, Athinai, Istanbul, Izmir, Bursa, Ankara, Erzurum, Halab, Dimashq, Bayrut, Jerusalem, El Iskandariya, El Qâhira, Makkah (Mecca), Al Madinah, El Khartûm, El Obeid, Port Sudan, Suakin, Addis Abeba, Harer, Juba, Mogadishu, Obbia, Djibouti, Zeila, Nairobi, Mombasa, Dar es Salaam, Kampala, Kisangani, Moskva, Leningrad, Murmansk, Arkhangelsk, Rostov, Odessa, Astrakhan, Baku, Tbilisi, Yerevan, Baghdad, Al Basrah, Tehrân, Esfahân, Shirâz, Tabriz, Mashhad, Ashkhabad, Bandar e Bushehr, Zâhedan, Muscat, Gwadar, Karachi, Quetta, Kandahâr, Kabul, Herât, Mary, Bukhoro, Samarkand, Tashkent, Alma Ata, Semipalatinsk, Omsk, Novosibirsk, Barnaul, Tomsk, Kemerovo, Krasnoyarsk, Irkutsk, Chita, Kyakhta, Yakutsk, Sverdlovsk, Chelyabinsk, Magnitogorsk, Orenburg, Khiva, Krasnovodsk, Ulan Bator (Ulaanbaatar), Hovd, Wulumuchi (Urumchi), Kashgar, Soche, Lhasa, Chengtu, Chungking, Kunming, Lanchow, Sian, Peiping, Tientsin, Tsingtao, Lu-ta, Shenyang (Mukden), Changchun, Harbin, Nanking, Wuhan, Shanghai, Soochow, Foochow, Canton, Hong Kong, Macau, Haikou, Hanoi, Phnôm Chi, Ho Chi Minh, Krung Thep, Mandalay, Myitkyina, Rangoon, Chittagong, Calcutta, Varanasi, Allahabad, Lucknow, Kanpur, Agra, Delhi, Lahore, Simla, Peshawar, Ahmadabad, Bombay, Hyderabad, Madras, Pondicherry, Calicut, Goa, Colombo, Manila, Davao, Mindanao, Zamboanga, Kuching, Kuala Lumpur, Singapore, Melaka, Jakarta, Kita-Kyushu, Nagasaki, Kagoshima, Osaka, Kyoto, Tokyo, Yokohama, Sapporo, Hakodate, Vladivostok, Khabarovsk, Nikolayevsk, Petropavlovsk, Petropavlovsk-Kamchatskiy

Rivers and Physical Features
Lena, Aldan, Amur, Ob, Irtysh, Yenisey, Tunguska, Angara, Volga, Don, Ural, Syr Darya, Tarim, Ining, Yarkand, Tsangpo, Mekong, Yangtze Kiang, Si Kiang, Hwang Ho, Irrawaddy, Salween, Ganges, Indus, Jumna, Narbada, Godavari, Brahmaputra, Nile, Tigris, Euphrates, Rhine, Danube, Wisła, Dnepr, Oder, Rhône
Ozero Baykal, Ozero Balkhash, Aral Sea
Urals
Himalaya
Kuen Lun

Islands
Aleutian Is.
Kurił Is.
Sakhalin
Hokkaido
Honshu
Kyushu
Shikoku
Ryukyu retto
Taiwan (Formosa)
Hainan
Luzon
Mindanao
Palawan
Borneo
Sumatera
Jawa
Sulawesi
Halmahera
Seram
Timor
Flores
Andaman Is. (India)
Nicobar Is. (India)
Sri Lanka (Ceylon)
Maldives
Lakshadweep Is. (India)
Socotra (South Yemen)
Svalbard
Novaya Zemlya
Severnaya Zemlya
Guam Is.
Caroline Is.
Palau Is.
Maluku (Moluccas)
Seychelles
Amirantes
Thursday I.
New Guinea

Shipping routes / distances
Vancouver 4282
San Francisco 4521
Honolulu 3379
Sydney 4316
Guam 1
Colombo – Fremantle 3120
Singapore 1630
Calcutta
Melbourne 6445
Aden – Melbourne

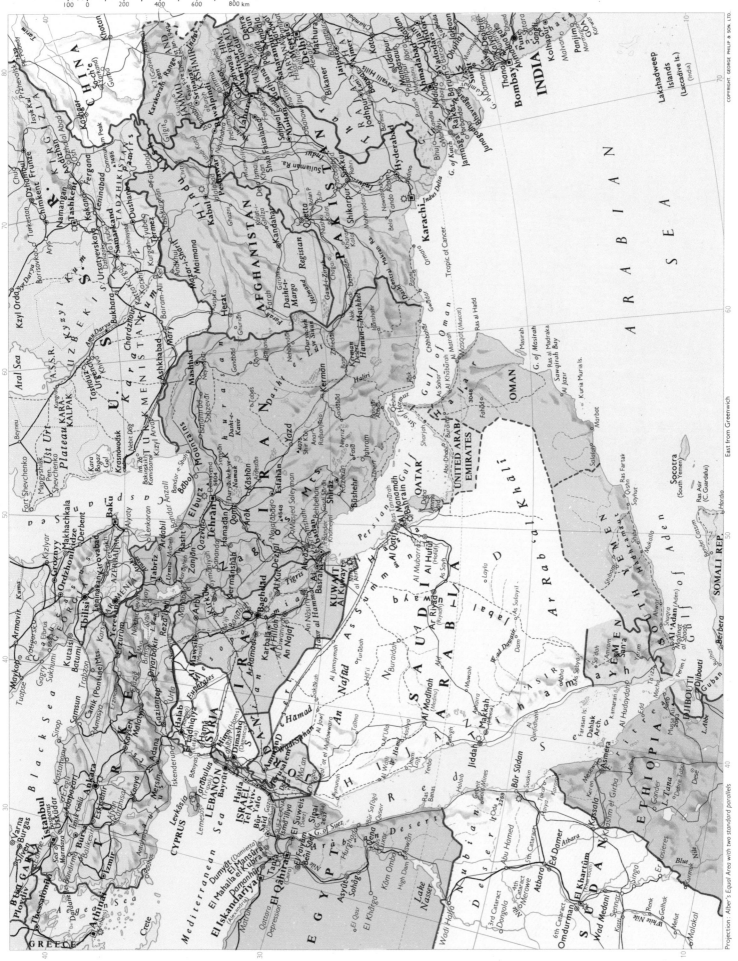

1:20 000 000

Projection: Alber's Equal Area with two standard parallels

East from Greenwich

1:20 000 000

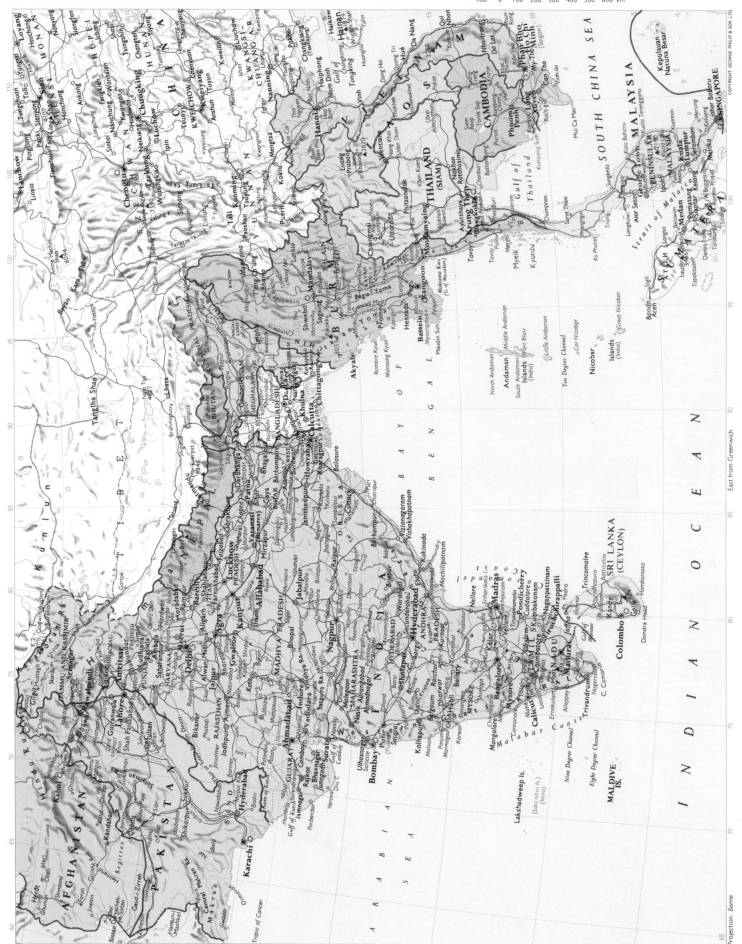

1:20 000 000

100   100   200   300   400   500 miles
100   0   200   400   600   800 km

P A C I F I C   O C E A N

Caroline Is.
Palau Is.
Caroline Islands
(U.S. Trust Territory)

Schouten Is.   Japen
Manokwari   Gelvink
Sorong   Vogelkop   IRIAN   JAYA
Misool   Fakfak
Waigeo
Gebe   Halmahera   Morotai
Ternate
MOLUCCAS   Obi Is.
Gt. Sangi   Gorontalo
Manado
CELEBES   SEA
SULAWESI (CELEBES)
Makasar   Str. of Makasar

A R A F U R A   S E A
Wessel Is.   C. Arnhem
Melville I.   Bathurst I.   Darwin
AUSTRALIA

C E R A M   S E A
Ceram   Ambon
B A N D A   S E A
Banda Is.
Buru   Namlea

T I M O R   S E A
Timor   Kupang
F L O R E S   S E A
Flores   Sumba (Sandalwood)   Savu

TAIWAN (FORMOSA)
Bashi Channel
Babuyan Chan.
Batan Is.   Babuyan Is.
Aparri
LUZON
Quezon City   MANILA
PHILIPPINES
Mindoro   Panay   Negros   Cebu   Bohol
SULU SEA
Palawan
Zamboanga   Basilan   Jolo
Mindanao   Davao   Davao Gulf
Surigao Strait   Samar   Leyte

S O U T H   C H I N A   S E A
Spratly   Paracel Is.   Con Son Is.
Natuna   Anambas Is.

CHINA
Hainan   Haikow   Changkiang
Kowloon   HONG KONG (Br.)   Victoria
Macau (Port.)

VIET-NAM
Hanoi   Haiphong   G. of Tongking
Hué (Tourane)   Da-Nang
Quang Tri   Qui Nhon   Nha Trang
PHAN BHO HO   PHAN THIET
HO CHI MINH (Saigon)

LAOS   Vientiane   Mekong
CAMBODIA   PHNOM PENH   Tonle Sap
THAILAND (SIAM)   KRUNG THEP (Bangkok)
Gulf   of   Thailand
Isthmus of Kra

BURMA   RANGOON   Bassein
Mouths of Irrawaddy
Moulmein   Amherst   Tavoy   Mergui
ANDAMAN   SEA
Andaman Islands (India)
Middle Andaman   Pt. Blair   Little Andaman
Nicobar Islands (India)
Great Nicobar   Car Nicobar
Ten Degree Channel

M A L A Y S I A
George Town   Penang   Ipoh   Kuala Lumpur   Seremban
SINGAPORE
Malacca   Strait of Malacca

B O R N E O   K A L I M A N T A N
SABAH   Kota Kinabalu   Kudat
BRUNEI   Miri   SARAWAK   Kuching   Sibu
Banjarmasin   Balikpapan   Pontianak

S U M A T R A
Banda Aceh (Kutaraja)   Medan   Padang   Palembang
Simeulue   Nias   Siberut   Mentawai Is.   Enggano
Bangka   Beliton

I N D O N E S I A
JAKARTA   BANDUNG   Semarang   SURABAJA
J A V A   Greater Sunda Islands
Bali   Lombok   Sumbawa   Sumba
Nusa Tenggara (Lesser Sunda Islands)

Christmas I. (Austral.)
Cocos or Keeling Is. (Austral.)

I N D I A N   O C E A N

Equator

East from Greenwich

Projection: Bonne

SEA OF JAPAN

PACIFIC OCEAN

SEA OF OKHOTSK

SOUTH KOREA

1:5 000 000

25	0				100 miles

25	0	50	100	150	km

Projection: Conical with two standard parallels

East from Greenwich

1:10 000 000

100	50	0	50	100	150	200 miles

100	0	100	200	300	km

Projection: Bonne

East from Greenwich

Continuation Southwards on same scale

Tokara-Kaikyō
Tokara-Shima
Nansei-Shoto
Amami-Ō-Shima
Toku-no-Shima
Ōsumi-Shotō
Tane-ga-Shima
Yaku-Shima
Suwanose-Jima

REFERENCE TO PREFECTURES

HOKKAIDŌ DISTRICT	
1	Hokkaidō

TŌHOKU DISTRICT	
2	Aomori
3	Akita
4	Iwate
5	Yamagata
6	Miyagi
7	Fukushima

CHŪBU DISTRICT	
8	Niigata
9	Ishikawa
10	Toyama
11	Fukui
12	Gifu
13	Nagano
14	Yamanashi
15	Aichi
16	Shizuoka

KANTO DISTRICT	
17	Gumma
18	Tochigi
19	Saitama
20	Ibaraki
21	Tōkyō
22	Chiba
23	Kanagawa

KINKI DISTRICT	
24	Hyogo
25	Kyōto
26	Shiga
27	Ōsaka
28	Nara
29	Mie
30	Wakayama

CHŪGOKU DISTRICT	
31	Tottori
32	Okayama
33	Shimane
34	Hiroshima
35	Yamaguchi

SHIKOKU DISTRICT	
36	Kagawa
37	Tokushima
38	Ehime
39	Kōchi

KYŪSHŪ DISTRICT	
40	Fukuoka
41	Saga
42	Nagasaki
43	Kumamoto
44	Ōita
45	Miyazaki
46	Kagoshima

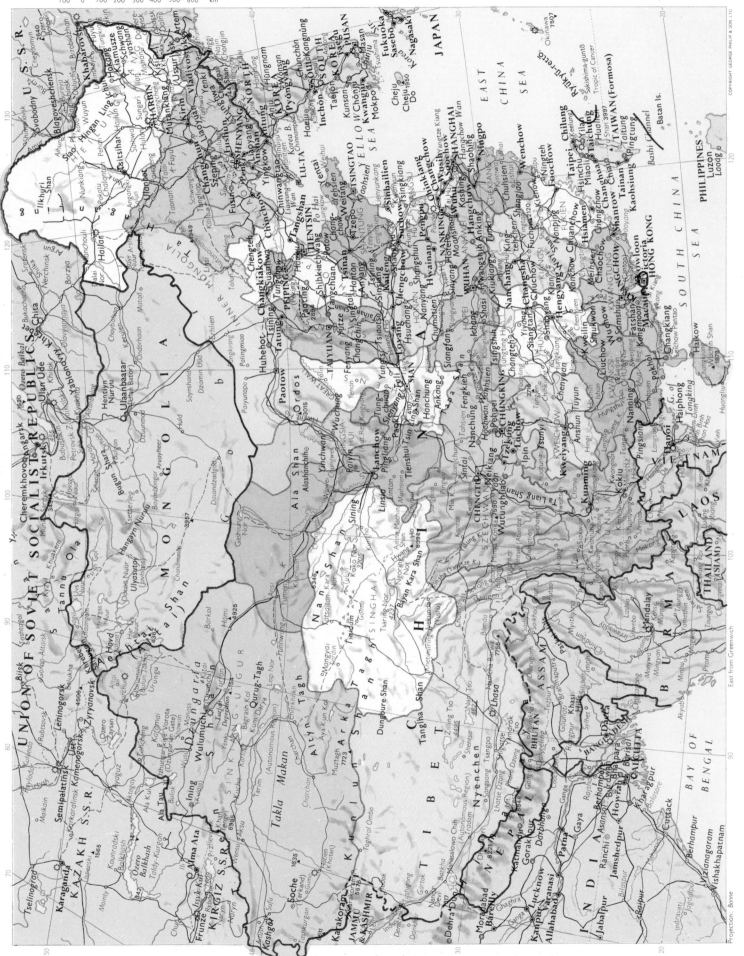

1:20 000 000

Projection: Bonne

Boundaries of the artesian basins

East from Greenwich

1:6 000 000

20 0 20 40 60 80 100 miles
20 0 40 80 120 160 km

NEW ZEALAND & DEPENDENCIES
1:60 000 000

200 0 200 400 600 800 miles
200 0 400 800 1200 km

- - - - - New Zealand Territory

Tokelau or Union Group
WESTERN SAMOA
Tutuila (U.S.)
Savaii
Upolu
Rotuma (Fiji)
Vanua Levu
FIJI
Viti Levu
Fiji Is.
Lau or Eastern Group
TONGA (Friendly Is.)
Niue
Pukapuka (Danger)
Nassau
Suwarrow
Rakahanga
Manihiki
Tongareva (Penrhyn) I.
Northern Group
Cook Is.
Palmerston Atoll
Aitutaki
Lower Group
Mitiaro Mauke
Rarotonga
Mangaia
Îles de la Société

Tropic of Capricorn

PACIFIC OCEAN

Raoul (Sunday) I.
Macauley
Curtis
Kermadec Is.

Three Kings Is.
Auckland
NORTH I.
NEW ZEALAND
SOUTH I.
Cook Strait
Wellington
Christchurch
Chatham I.
Chatham Is.
Pitt I.
Tasman Sea
Dunedin
Bounty Is.
Stewart I.
Antipodes Is.
Snares
Campbell I.
Auckland Is.
Macquarie I. (Austr.)

SOUTHERN OCEAN

NORTH ISLAND

Three Kings Is.
North C.
C. Reinga
C. Maria var. Diemen
Houhora
Rangaunu Bay
Doubtless Bay
Aniwa B.
Kaitaia
Mangonui
Whangaroa Harb.
Reef Pt.
Rawene
B. of Islands
Opua
C. Brett
Hokianga Harb.
Kaikohe
Donnelly's Crossing
Hikurangi
Whangarei
Whangarei Harb.
Bream Hd.
Bream Bay
Dargaville
Waipu
Kaipara Harb.
Lit. Barrier I.
C. Rodney
Gt. Barrier I.
Warkworth
Cuvier I.
C. Colville
Helensville
Hauraki Gulf
C.Colville
Coromandel
Whitianga
Takapuna
Devonport
Mt. Eden
AUCKLAND
Onehunga
Manukau
Papakura
Thames
Glenbrook
Mercer
Waiuku
Pukekohe
Mayor I.
Waihi
Waikato
Huntly
Paeroa
Tauranga Harb.
Te Aroha
Waihi
Raglan
Morrinsville
Tauranga
Bay of Plenty
Kawhia Harb.
Hamilton
Cambridge
Te Puke
Whakatane
Opotiki
Te Awamutu
Putaruru
Kawerau
Raukumara Ra.
Otorohanga
L.Roto
Rotorua
Murupara
Hikurangi 753
Te Kuiti
Mokai
Wairakei
FOREST
Waioeka
Waipiro
Moutohora
Ongarue
Taupo
L.Taupo
Taneatua
Ormond
Toluga
North Taranaki Bight
Taumarunui
Ruatahuna
Waikaremoana
Gisborne
New Plymouth
Inglewood
Waitara
Wanganomoana
Waimarino
Kaimanawa Mts.
Nuhaka
Poverty Bay
Mt. Egmont 2518
Stratford
Eltham
Ruapehu 2796
Raetihi
Waiouru
Wairoa
Opunake
Kaponi
Ohakune
Waimarino
Mahia Peninsula
Hawke Bay
South Taranaki Bight
Hawera
Waverley
Taihape
Mangaweka
Runanga
Napier
C. Kidnappers
Pateo
Hastings
Wanganui
Marton
Bulls
Halcombe
Waipukurau
Palmerston N.
Feilding
Dannevirke
Foxton
Shannon
Woodville
Pahiatua
Levin
Eketahuna
Otaki
Te Horo
C. Turnagain
Kapiti I.
Paraparaumu
Featherston
Masterton
Up. Hutt
Greytown
Martinborough
Petone
Lr. Hutt
WELLINGTON
Eastbourne
Castle Pt.
WELLINGTON
Cook Strait

PACIFIC OCEAN

SOUTH ISLAND

TASMAN SEA

C. Farewell
Golden Bay
D'Urville I.
Collingwood
Takaka
Tasman Bay
French Pass
Pelorus
Tasman Mts.
Motueka
Te Horo
Picton
Karamea Bight
Nelson
Richmond
Havelock
Blenheim
Seddonville
Wakefield
Tadmor
Wairau
Granity
Lyell Ra.
Murchison
Rotoroa
Seddon
Ward
Westport
Inangahua Junction
2885 Tapuaenuku
MARLBOROUGH
Reefton
L.Rotoiti
Kaikoura
Blackball
Ahaura
Spenser Mts.
Hanmer
2337 Mt. Travers
Clarence
Greymouth
Brunner
Amuri P.
Kaikoura
Kumara
L. Brunner
Jacksons
Hokitika
Oura Gorge
Waikari
Ross
Arthur's Pass
Beoley
Waipara
Culverden
Waiau
Amberley
Pegasus Bay
Okarito
Abut Hd.
Rangiora
Oxford
Kaiapoi
New Brighton
Springfield
Waimakariri
Christchurch
Riccarton
Lyttelton
Methven
Lincoln
Banks Peninsula
Mt. Cook 3764
Springburn
Little River
Akaroa
Southern Alps
Tekapo
Rakaia
L. Ellesmere
Hermitage
Fairlie
Ashburton
Canterbury Plains
Mt. Aspiring 3035
L. Pukaki
Canterbury Bight
Waimate
Temuka
Timaru
Jackson B.
Haast
Milford Sd.
Mt. Earnslaw 2819
L. Wanaka
L. Hawea
St. Andrews
George Sd.
Wanaka
Kurow
Waimate
Bligh Sd.
Sutherland Falls
Kinloch
Cromwell
Naseby
Ngapara
Secretary I.
Queenstown
Arrowtown
Clyde
Maheno
Oamaru
Doubtful Sd.
Te Anau
Kingston
Alexandra
Hampden
Breaksea Sd.
Manapouri
Garvie Mts.
Roxburgh
Dunback
Palmerston
Resolution I.
Lumsden
Edievale
Kelso
Port Chalmers
Dusky Sd.
Mossburn
Tapanui
Otago Harbour
Ohai
Lawrence
Green Island
St. Kilda
Chalky Inlet
Clifden
Nightcaps
Milton
Dunedin
Preservation Inlet
Tuatapere
Gore
Clinton
Mosgiel
C. Saunders
Orepuki
Riverton
Winton
Balclutha
Kaitangata
Invercargill
Wyndham
Mataura
Nugget Pt.
Bluff
Owaka
Ruapuke I.
Foveaux Str.
Oban
Stewart I.
S.W. Cape
Port Pegasus

SAMOA ISLANDS
1:12 000 000

WESTERN SAMOA
Savaii
Apia
Upolu
American Samoa
Pago Pago
Manua Is.
Rose I.
Tutuila

FIJI AND TONGA ISLANDS
1:12 000 000

50 0 50 100 150 miles
50 0 50 100 150 200 250 km

Futuna (Fr.)
Niuafo'ou (Tonga)
Thikombia
Lambása
Vanua Levu
Taveuni
FIJI
Yasawa Group
Koro
Lautoka
Levuka
Ovalau
Lau or Eastern Group
Nandi
Viti Levu 1323
Koro Sea
Lakemba
Suva
Ngau
Vanua Mbalavu
Moala
Kandavu
Moala
TONGA
Tonga (Friendly) Is.
Vatoa
Vava'u
Tofua I.
Tongatapu
Nuku'alofa

Projection: Conical with two standard parallels

COPYRIGHT. GEORGE PHILIP & SON, LTD.

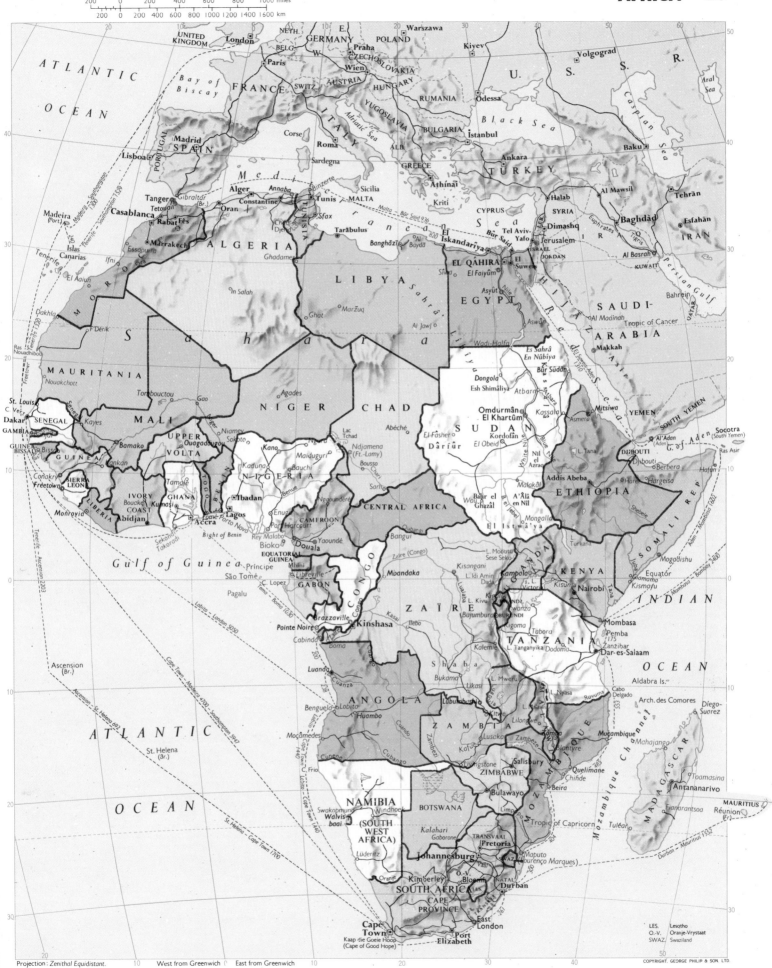

1:40 000 000

200   0   200   400   600   800   1000 miles
200   0   200 400 600 800 1000 1200 1400 1600 km

ATLANTIC OCEAN

UNITED KINGDOM   London

NETH.   GERMANY   E.   POLAND   Warszawa

BELG.   W.   Kiyev

Bay of Biscay   Paris   CZECHOSLOVAKIA   Praha

FRANCE   SWITZ.   AUSTRIA   HUNGARY   RUMANIA   Odessa   U.   S.   S.   R.

Volgograd

Corse   Wien   YUGOSLAVIA   BULGARIA   Istanbul   Black Sea   Aral Sea

Madrid   ITALY   Roma   Adriatic Sea   Athínai   Ankara   TURKEY   Baku   Caspian Sea

SPAIN   Sardegna   GREECE   Kriti   CYPRUS   SYRIA   Halab   Al Mawsil   Tehrān

Lisboa   PORTUGAL   Sicilia   MALTA   Tel Aviv-Yafo   Dimashq   Baghdād   Esfahān

Tanger   Gibraltar (Br.)   Alger   Annaba   Tunis   Malta   El Iskandariya   Jerusalem   IRAN

Casablanca   Tetouan   Oran   Constantine   TUNISIA   Sfax   Banghāzī   Bayda   El Qāhira   El Suweis   Al Basrah

Rabat   Fès   Djelfa   El Faiyûm   JORDAN   KUWAIT   Persian Gulf

Marrakech   ALGERIA   LIBYA   EGYPT   Tropic of Cancer   SAUDI-ARABIA   Bahrein   QATAR

Essaouira   Ghadames   Al Madinah

Ifni   In Salah   Ghat   Marzûq   Al Jawf   Aswân   Makkah

El Aaiun   Dakhla   S   a   h   a   r   a   Wadi-Halfa   Es Sahrâ En Nûbiya

Ras Nouadhibou   Nouakchott   MAURITANIA   Agades   Dongola   Esh Shimâliya   Bûr Sûdân   YEMEN

Tombouctou   Gao   NIGER   CHAD   Omdurmân   El Khartûm   Kassala   Mitsiwa   Al'Adan   SOUTH YEMEN   Socotra (South Yemen)

St. Louis   C. Vert   Dakar   SENEGAL   Kayes   MALI   Niamey   Abéché   SUDAN   Kordofân   Asmera   DJIBOUTI   Djibouti   Ras Asir

GAMBIA   Bamako   UPPER VOLTA   Ouagadougou   Kano   Ndjamena (Ft.-Lamy)   El Fâsher   Dârfûr   El Obeid   Berbera

GUINEA BISSAU   Bissau   GUINEA   Kankan   Kaduna   Maiduguri   Bousso   ETHIOPIA   Hargeisa

Conakry   Freetown   SIERRA LEONE   Bauchi   NIGERIA   Addis Abeba   SOMALI REP.

LIBERIA   IVORY COAST   GHANA   Ibadan   Enugu   CENTRAL AFRICA   Bangui   El Istwâ'ya   Mongalla

Monrovia   Bouaké   Kumasi   Lagos   Cameroon   Yaoundé   Bangui   Juba   Mogadishu

Abidjan   Accra   Porto Novo   Port Harcourt   Douala   EQUATORIAL GUINEA   ZAÏRE   Kisangani   KENYA   Equator   INDIAN

Sekondi-Takoradi   Bight of Benin   Rey Malabo   São Tomé   GABON   Libreville   Mbandaka   UGANDA   Nairobi   Kismayu   OCEAN

Gulf of Guinea   Príncipe   Mbini   Kampala   Mombasa

Pagalu   CONGO   Brazzaville   Kinshasa   Kigali   RWANDA   BURUNDI   TANZANIA   Pemba

Ascension (Br.)   Pointe Noire   Cabinda   Boma   Kasai   Ilebo   Bujumbura   Tabora   Dodoma   Zanzibar   Dar-es-Salaam

ATLANTIC   Luanda   Shaba   Bukama   Kalemie   L. Tanganyika   OCEAN

St. Helena (Br.)   ANGOLA   Benguela   Lobito   Huambo   Likasi   Lubumbashi   L. Mweru   Aldabra Is.

Moçamedes   ZAMBIA   Lusaka   L. Nyasa   Arch. des Comores   Diego-Suarez

OCEAN   NAMIBIA (SOUTH WEST AFRICA)   Windhoek   BOTSWANA   ZIMBABWE   Salisbury   Bulawayo   MOZAMBIQUE   Beira   MADAGASCAR   Antananarivo   MAURITIUS   Réunion (Fr.)

Swakopmund   Walvis baai   Kalahari   Gaborone   Livingstone   TRANSVAAL   Pretoria   SWAZ.   Maputo (Lourenço Marques)   Toamasina

Lüderitz   Johannesburg   Kimberley   Bloemfontein   O.V.   NATAL   Durban

Oranje   SOUTH AFRICA   CAPE PROVINCE   East London

Cape Town   Kaap die Goeie Hoop (Cape of Good Hope)   Port Elizabeth

LES.   Lesotho
O.-V.   Oranje-Vrystaat
SWAZ.   Swaziland

Projection: Zenithal Equidistant.   West from Greenwich   East from Greenwich   COPYRIGHT. GEORGE PHILIP & SON. LTD.

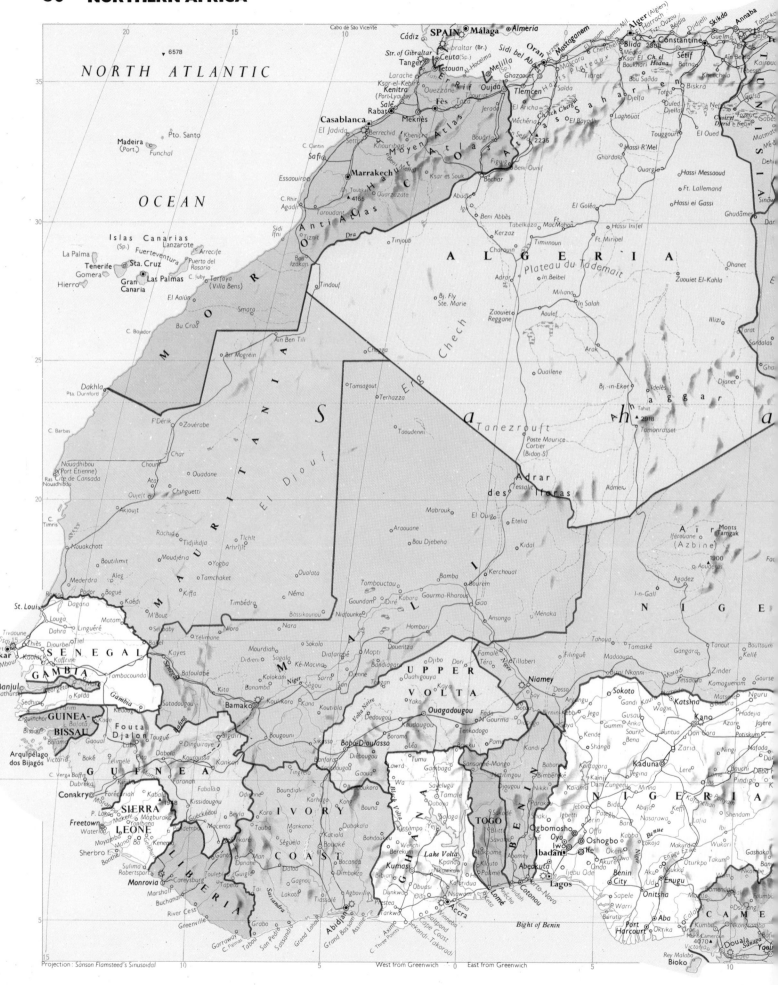

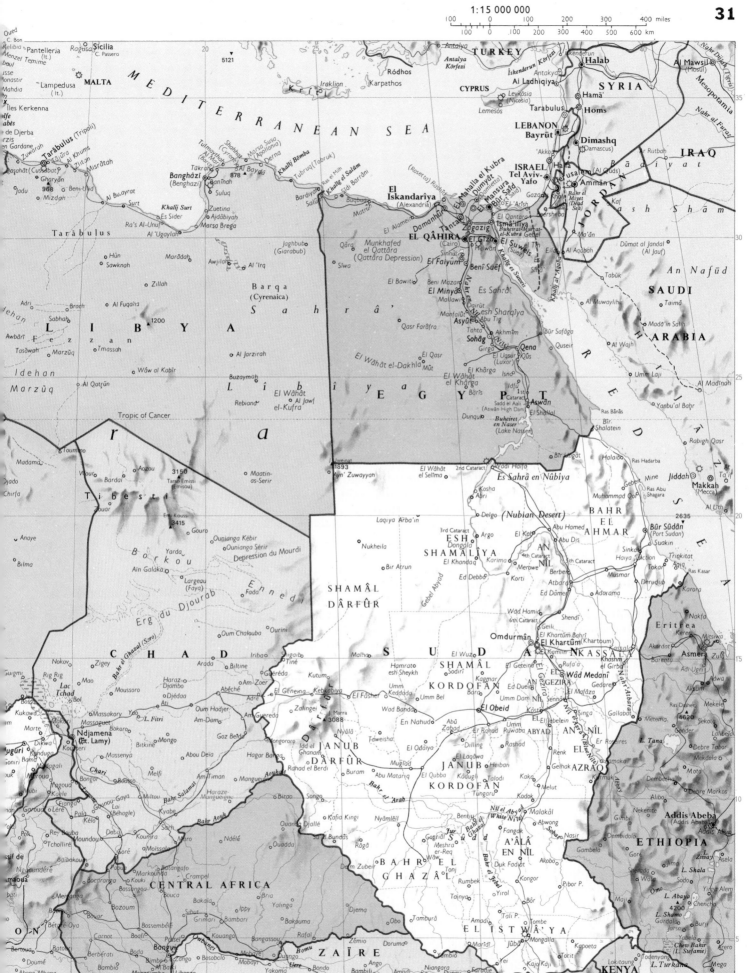

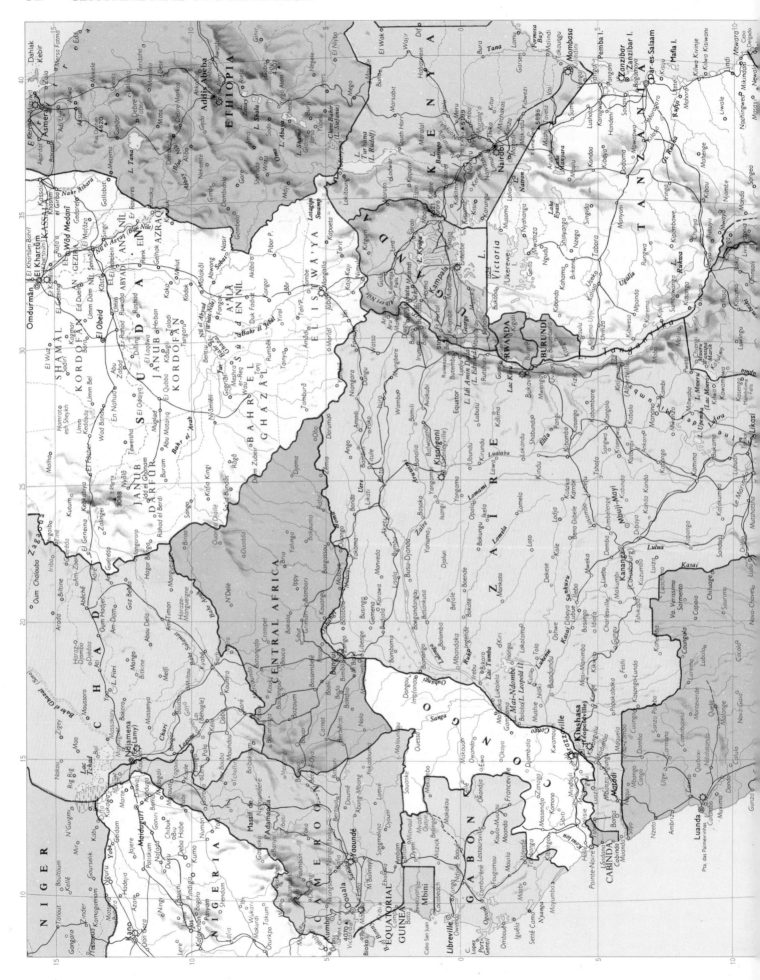

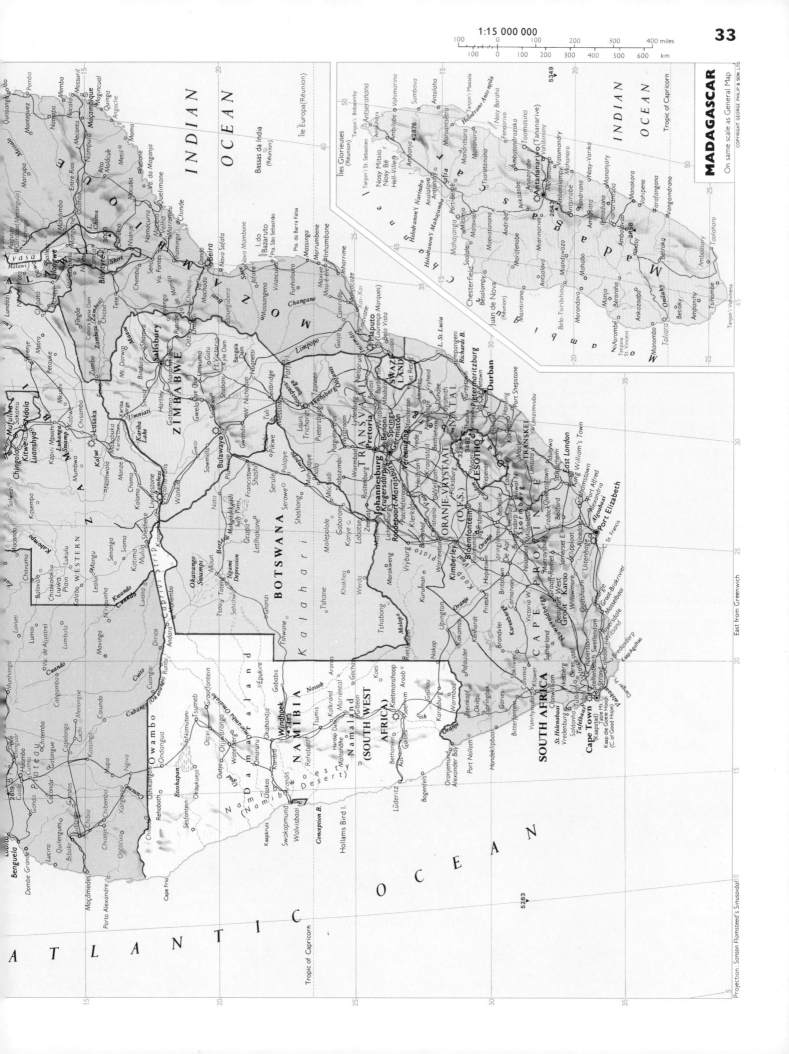

Projection: Bonne

ALASKA
1:30 000 000
100 0   100 200 300 miles
100 0   200   400 km

West from Greenwich

1:15 000 000

100   50   0   200   300   400 miles
100   0   100   200   300   400   500   600 km

Devon Island
Lancaster Sound

Baffin Bay

G R E E N L A N D

A T L A N T I C

Brodeur
Peninsula
Arctic Bay
Bylot I.
Pond Inlet
Scott I.
Clyde

Disko
Egedesminde
Christianshåb

Sukkertoppen

Kong Frederik VIII's Kyst

Fury & Hecla Str.
Igloolik
Island
Hall
Lake

Davis Strait
Home B.
Broughton
Island
Padloping Island
C. Dyer
Cape
Dyer
Holsteinsborg

Sndre Strømfjord

Gotthåb

Frederikshåb

Pelly
Bay
Melville
Peninsula
Prince
Charles
I.
Foxe

Cumberland
Peninsula
Pangnirtung
Hoare B.
C. Mercy

Nanortalik
Kap Farvel

Rae Isthmus
Repulse
Bay
Foxe
Basin
Nettilling
L.
Cumberland Sd.

Roes Welcome Sd.
Southampton
I.
Coral Harbour
C. Dorchester
Foxe
Penin.
Amadjuak
L.
Frobisher
Bay
C. Chidley

Wager
B.
Bell
Pen.
Coats
I.
Cape Dorset
Amadjuak
Lake
Harbour
Frobisher Bay
Resolution I.

Digges Is.
Sugluk
(Saglouk)
Ivugivik
(Notre-Dame
d'Ivugivic)
Maricourt
(Wakeham
Bay)
Koartac
Notre Dame
de Koartac
Akpatok
I.

Hudson Strait

Mansel
I.

Bellin
Payne Bay
Payne
Ungava Bay
Port Nouveau-Québec
George R.
Hebron

H u d s o n

Ungava
Peninsula

Payne L.
Leaf
Larch
Ft. Chimo
Loksoak
George
Whale
Nutak
Nain

Ottawa
Is.
257

Portland
Promontory
Peninsula
Kaniapiskau
Hopedale

Bay

Inoucdjouac
(Port Harrison)

L. Minto
Lower Seal L.

Harrison
Indian Harbour

Sleeper Is.
King
George Is.
King George Is.
Baker's
Dozen

Clearwater
Lac Bienville
Scheffeville
Petitsikapau
Michikamau
L.
Rigolet

L A B R A D O R

Belcher
Is.
Gr. Whale
to Baleine
(Great Whale River)
Obstick L.
Churchill
Falls
North West R.
Cartwright

C. Henrietta
Maria
C. Jones
Fort George
Ft. George
Kaniapiskau
L.
Ashuanipi
Wabush City
Churchill
Romaine
Battle Harb.
Belle Isle

Winisk
James Bay
Akimiski
I.
Nouveau Comptoir
(Paint Hills)
Eastmain
1128
Gagnon
Notashquan

Notre Dame B.
Twillingate

Big
Trout L.
Attawapiskat
East Main
Fort George
Q U E B E C
Moisie
Mingan
Anticosti
Gander

N E W F O U N D L A N D
Bonavista
Trinity B.
St. John's

Ft. Albany
Charlton
Fort Rupert
(Rupert
House)
Rupert
Mistassini
L. Albanel
Péribonca
Sept Iles
Port Cartier
Magdalen Is.
Trepassey
C. Race

Albany
Moosonee
Chibougamau
Baie Comeau
R. St. Lawrence
Gaspé
C. Gaspé
Gulf of
St. Lawrence
Cabot Str.
ST. PIERRE
et MIQUELON
(Fr.)

Nakina
Longlac
Hearst
Gouin
Reservoir
Dolbeau
Betsiamites
Matane
Gaspé Pen.
Rimouski
Campbellton
PR. EDWARD I.
Summerside
Charlottetown
Cape
North
Sydney
Glace Bay

Nipigon
Cochrane
Abitibi
Taschereau
Senneterre
Doucet
Weymont
Roberval
Saguenay
Rivière
du Loup
Edmundston
Newcastle
Chatham
Bathurst
Moncton
Amherst
Springhill
Pictou
New Glasgow

Thunder Bay
(Ft. William)
Michipicoten
Timmins
Norand
Rouyn
La Tuque
Shawinigan
Chicoutimi
1190
St. Léonard
NEW
BRUNSWICK
Sackville
Windsor
Truro
Dartmouth
Port Hawkesbury
C. Canso

Longlac
Heron Bay
Oba
Franz
Kirkland Lake
Val d'Or
Québec
Levis
Thetford Mines
Woodstock
Fredericton
Saint
John
NOVA
SCOTIA
Halifax
Bridgewater

Michipicoten Hr.
Cobalt
Timiskaming
Cabonga
Reservoir
Shawinigan
Trois Rivières
Joliette
Sorel
St. Hyacinthe
Sherbrooke
Bangor
M A I N E
Augusta
Bridgewater
Liverpool
Shelburne
C. Sable
Yarmouth

Sault Ste. Marie
Sudbury
Copper cliff
North
Bay
Ottawa
Hull
MONTREAL
Lachine
L. Champlain
VERMONT
NEW
HAMPSHIRE
B. of Fundy

Georgian
Bay
Parry
Sound
Pembroke
Arnprior
Ottawa
Cornwall
1917
Lewiston
Portland
Manchester
Concord
Lowell
Boston
C. Cod

TORONTO
Guelph
Ontario
Orillia
Peterboro
Belleville
Kingston
Watertown
Glens
Falls
Albany
Worcester
MASS.
Providence

London
Hamilton
Brantford
Niagara
Falls
Buffalo
Rochester
Syracuse
Utica
Springfield
CONN.
New Haven

DETROIT
Windsor
Erie
Cleveland
Youngstown
Williamsport
Scranton
Wilkes Barre
Binghamton
Waterbury
Bridgeport
New York

CHICAGO
Gary
South Bend
Toledo
Akron
OHIO
PENNSYLVANIA
Allentown
Reading
Trenton
NEW JERSEY
Newark
NEW YORK
Jersey City

West from Greenwich
COPYRIGHT. GEORGE PHILIP & SON. LTD.

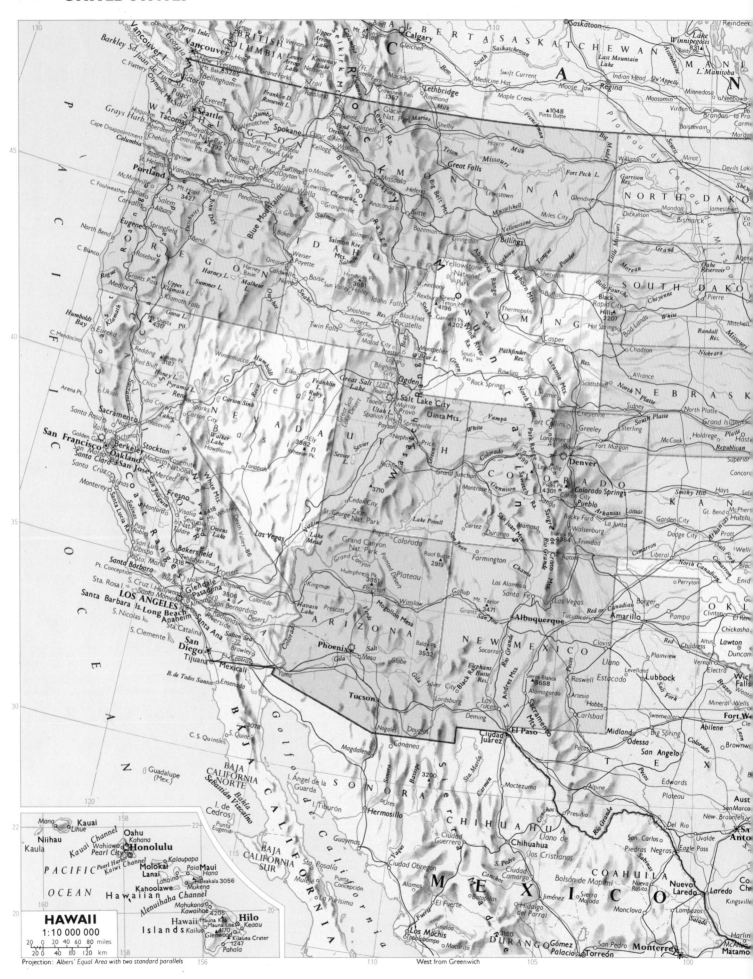

HAWAII
1:10 000 000
20 0 20 40 60 80 miles
20 0 40 60 120 km

Projection: Albers' Equal Area with two standard parallels

West from Greenwich

1:12 000 000

COPYRIGHT. GEORGE PHILIP & SON. LTD

1:12 000 000

REFERENCE TO NUMBERS
1 Distrito Federal   5 México
2 Aguascalientes   6 Morelos
3 Guanajuato   7 Querétaro
4 Hidalgo   8 Tlaxcala

PANAMA CANAL
1:1 000 000

Projection: Bi-polar oblique Conical Orthomorphic

West from Greenwich

U N I T E D   S T A T E S

G U L F   O F   M E X I C O

P A C I F I C   O C E A N

Bahía de Campeche

GUATEMALA

BELIZE

HONDURAS

SALVADOR

Tropic of Cancer

Gulf of Tehuantepec

NEW ORLEANS
BIRMINGHAM
Montgomery
Little Rock
DALLAS
FORT WORTH
SAN ANTONIO
HOUSTON
Austin
Corpus Christi
Galveston
Baton Rouge
Shreveport
El Paso
Ciudad Juárez
Chihuahua
Phoenix
Tucson
SAN DIEGO
Tijuana
Mexicali
Hermosillo
Ciudad Obregón
Culiacán
Mazatlán
La Paz
Durango
Torreón
Gómez Palacio
Monterrey
Saltillo
Nuevo Laredo
Laredo
Matamoros
Brownsville
Harlingen
Reynosa
Tampico
Ciudad Madero
Ciudad Victoria
San Luis Potosí
Aguascalientes
GUADALAJARA
Morelia
León
Irapuato
Querétaro
MÉXICO
Puebla
Pachuca
Toluca
Veracruz
Jalapa
Oaxaca
Acapulco
Chilpancingo
Mérida
Campeche
Chetumal

BAJA CALIFORNIA
BAJA CALIFORNIA SUR
SONORA
CHIHUAHUA
COAHUILA
DURANGO
SINALOA
NAYARIT
JALISCO
ZACATECAS
NUEVO LEÓN
TAMAULIPAS
SAN LUIS POTOSÍ
MICHOACÁN
GUERRERO
OAXACA
VERACRUZ
CHIAPAS
TABASCO
CAMPECHE
YUCATÁN
QUINTANA ROO

Sierra Madre

G u l f   o f   C a l i f o r n i a

PANAMA
REPUBLIC OF PANAMA
Colón
PANAMÁ
Gatún Locks
Gatún Dam
Madden Dam
Miraflores Locks
Pedro Miguel Locks
ATLANTIC OCEAN
PACIFIC OC.

COPYRIGHT GEORGE PHILIP & SON, LTD.

1:12 000 000

100 0 100 200 miles
100 0 100 200 300 km

WINDWARD ISLANDS
1:8 000 000

0 25 50 miles
0 20 40 60 80 km

TRINIDAD & TOBAGO
1:8 000 000

JAMAICA
1:8 000 000

LEEWARD ISLANDS
1:8 000 000

BERMUDA
1:1 000 000

0 5 miles
0 8 km

St. George's I.
St. David's I.
Castle Harb.
Spanish Flatts
North Village
Hamilton
The Spanish Flatts
Ireland I.
Somerset
Somerset I.

BARBADOS
Speightstown
Bridgetown

ST. LUCIA
Castries

MARTINIQUE
Fort-de-France

ST. VINCENT
Kingstown

GRENADA
St. George's

Barbuda
ANTIGUA
St. John's
Montserrat
GUADELOUPE
Basse Terre
DOMINICA
Roseau

Anguilla
St. Martin (Fr.)
St. Barthélemy (Fr.)
Saba (Neth.)
St. Christopher
Nevis
St. Eustatius (Neth.)

Port of Spain
TRINIDAD
San Fernando

KINGSTON
Montego Bay

ATLANTIC OCEAN

GULF OF MEXICO

FLORIDA
Miami
Fort Lauderdale
Key West
Palm Beach
Fort Pierce
Vero Beach

BAHAMAS
GREAT BAHAMA BANK
Nassau
Andros Island
New Providence
Eleuthera I.
Cat I.
Long I.
Crooked I.
Acklins I.
Great Inagua I.
Little Inagua I.
Mayaguana I.
Caicos Islands
Turks I.

CUBA
La Habana
Marianao
Matanzas
Cárdenas
Santa Clara
Cienfuegos
Sancti Spíritus
Camagüey
Holguín
Santiago de Cuba
Guantánamo
Pinar del Río

Cayman Islands (Br.)
Grand Cayman

JAMAICA
KINGSTON
Montego Bay
Spanish Town

HAITI
Port-au-Prince
Gonaïves
Cap-Haïtien

DOMINICAN REP.
Santo Domingo
Santiago
San Pedro de Macorís
Barahona

HISPANIOLA

PUERTO RICO (U.S.A.)
San Juan
Ponce
Mayagüez
Arecibo

Virgin Is.

CARIBBEAN SEA

GREATER ANTILLES

LESSER ANTILLES

Aruba (Neth.)
Curaçao (Neth.)
Bonaire (Neth.)

VENEZUELA
CARACAS
Maracaibo
Barquisimeto
Valencia
Barcelona
Cumaná
Maturín
Ciudad Bolívar
Isla Margarita
Los Roques
La Orchila
La Blanquilla
Los Testigos
La Tortuga

COLOMBIA
BARRANQUILLA
Cartagena
Santa Marta
Bucaramanga

Archipiélago de las Mulatas
I. de Providencia (Colombia)
I. de San Andrés (Colombia)
Golfo de Darién

PANAMA
Colón
Panamá

COSTA RICA
San José
Limón

NICARAGUA
Managua
León
Granada
Bluefields
Lago de Nicaragua

HONDURAS
Tegucigalpa
Islas de la Bahía
Swan Islands (U.S.A.)

MEXICO
Isla de Cozumel
C. Catoche

PACIFIC OCEAN

West from Greenwich

Projection: Bi-polar oblique Conical Orthomorphic

1:16 000 000

100   0   100   200   300   400   500 miles
100   0   100   200   300   400   500   600   700   800 km

A T L A N T I C

Amsterdam
Nickerie
lotnets
Paramaribo Nieuw Amsterdam
Wickerie Mana
wakaegras St. Laurent Iracoubo
Brakopondo Albina Sinnamary
Kaw Approuague
RINAM St. Georges Cayenne
Kabalebo C. Orange
FR. St. Georges Oiapoque
GUIANA Camopi
Coppename Amapá
Serra Tumucumaque Jari Ilha de Maracá
Meriruma AMAPÁ C. do Norte
Cumaú Araguari
Ferru Serra Pta. Grande
Serra do Navio
Mazagão Estuario do
I. Grande Rio Amazonas
Monte Alegre Pralinha Almeirim Macapá Ilha Caviana
Óbidos Gurupá Ilha Mexiana
Juruti Santarém Breves Ilha de C. Maguarinho
Brasília Legal Porto de Moz Marajó Chaves
Itaituba Aveiro Afuá Vigia Salinópolis
Belterra Altamira Sousel Curuçá Bragança
nás Itaituba Baião Muaná Igarapé Açu Viseu
Cametá Abaetetuba Belém (Pará) Turiaçu Cururupu
Acará Turiaçu São Luís (Maranhão)
P A R Á Curralinho Guimarães B. de São Marcos
Tocantins Jacundá Rosário Alcântara
Tucuruí Abaetetuba Brejo de Barreirinhas Tutóia
Marabá Itapecuru- Parnaíba Luís Correia
São João Mirim Camocim
do Araguaia Barra do Caxias Granja Fortaleza (Ceará)
Imperatriz Corda Codó União Ipu Sobral
Conceição do MARANHÃO Teresina Maranguape
Araguaia Grajaú Coroatá Piripiri Batuité Aracati
Araguacema Tocantinópolis Caxias Crateús Quixadá Macau
Riachão Colinas Amarante Oeiras CEARÁ Mossoró RIO GRANDE
Pedro Afonso Loreto Valença do Piauí Iguatu Limoeiro DO NORTE C. de São Roque
Sta. Filomena Floriano Icó Iço Natal
Conceição do Novalorque Oeiras Crato Cedro Nova Cruz
Araguaia São João Juazeiro do Norte PARAÍBA Canguaretama
PIAUÍ do Piauí Cajazeiras Campina Grande Mamanguape
Caracol Dois Irmãos São Raimundo Patos João Pessoa
Remanso Casa Nova Petrolândia Arcoverde (Paraíba)
Pernaguá PERNAMBUCO Caruaru RECIFE
Juàzeiro Paulo Afonso (Pernambuco)
Xique-Xique Campo Garanhuns Pta. de Santo Antão
Formoso Senhor do Palmares
Barra Bonfim ALAGOAS Maceió
GOIÁS Queimadas Pal dos Índios
Porto Nacional Jacobina Capela SERGIPE Penedo
Natividade Feira de Propriá Aracajú
Peixe Paraná Santana São Cristóvão
Paranã Barreiras Estância
Campos Belos Paratinga B A H I A Alagoinhas
São Domingos Itaberaba Santo Amaro
Sta. Maria Bom Jesus Itaeté Salvador (Bahia)
da Vitória da Lapa 1850 Sincorá Valença
Niquelândia Caetité Ituaçu Jequié
Aruanã 1678 Carinhanha Brumado Ubaitaba
Condeúba Ilhéus
DIST. Formoso Monte Azul Vitória da Itabuna
FED. Brasília Januária Conquista Canavieiras
Anápolis Vianópolis Belmonte
Goiânia Buziânia Montes São Francisco Porto Seguro
Vianópolis Claros Salinas
Morrinhos Paracatu Pirapora Pedra Azul Jequitinhonha
Catalão Diamantina Araçuaí
Rio Verde Patos de Teófilo Otoni Nanuque Prado
Itumbiara Minas Caravelas
MINAS GERAIS Gov. Valadares Mucuri Abrolhos
Uberaba Araxá Belo Horizonte Aimorés Conceição da Barra
Uberlândia Ipatinga Nova São Mateus
Franca Ouro Preto Venécia Vitória
Prata Pico da Cachoeiro de Itapemirim
SÃO Ribeirão Preto Bandeira 2891
Marília PAULO Poços de Juiz de Fora Campos
Bauru Caldas Petrópolis
Piracicaba Campinas RIO DE JANEIRO Niterói
Botucatu RIO DE JANEIRO

Equator

O C E A N

Fernando de Noronha
(Braz.)

Rocas

6059

Trindade
(Braz.)

1:16 000 000

100 50 0 100 200 300 miles
100 0 100 200 300 400 km

SOUTH ATLANTIC OCEAN

PARAGUAY

BRAZIL

SÃO PAULO

RIO DE JANEIRO

Curitiba

Paranaguá

São Francisco do Sul

Joinvile

SANTA CATARINA

Blumenau

Florianópolis

Lajes

Criciúma

Tubarão

Laguna

RIO GRANDE DO SUL

Caxias do Sul

Pôrto Alegre

Pelotas

Rio Grande

Lagoa dos Patos

Asunción

Villarrica

Concepción

Formosa

Resistencia

Corrientes

Posadas

Encarnación

Santiago del Estero

Catamarca

San Miguel de Tucumán

Salta

S. Salvador de Jujuy

Antofagasta

Tocopilla

Tropic of Capricorn

La Rioja

San Juan

Córdoba

Santa Fe

Paraná

Rosario

URUGUAY

Artigas

Rivera

Paysandú

Salto

Concordia

Mercedes

MONTEVIDEO

BUENOS AIRES

La Plata

Avellaneda

Mar del Plata

Bahía Blanca

Santa Rosa

Mendoza

San Luis

Río Cuarto

Villa María

Viña del Mar

Valparaíso

SANTIAGO

Rancagua

San Fernando

Curicó

Talca

Linares

Chillán

Concepción

Talcahuano

Coronel

Los Ángeles

Temuco

Valdivia

Osorno

Puerto Montt

Ancud

I. de Chiloé

Archipiélago de los Chonos

Carlos de Bariloche

Neuquén

Viedma

Golfo San Matías

Península Valdés

Golfo Nuevo

Trelew

Rawson

Comodoro Rivadavia

Golfo San Jorge

C. Dos Bahías

PATAGONIA

Río Gallegos

Punta Arenas

Estrecho de Magallanes (Magellan's Str.)

Tierra del Fuego

Cabo de Hornos (C. Horn)

Beagle Canal

FALKLAND ISLANDS (ISLAS MALVINAS) (Br.)

West Falkland

East Falkland

Stanley

Darwin

Falkland Sound

South Georgia (Br.)

Peru-Chile Trench

ABBREVIATIONS

Afghan. – *Afghanistan*
Afr. – *Africa*
Alas. – *Alaska*
Alg. – *Algeria*
Amer. – *America*
Ang. – *Angola*
Ant. – *Antarctica*
Arch. – *Archipelago*
Arg. – *Argentina*
Austral. – *Australia*
B. – *Bay, Bight (Baie, Bahia, Baia)*
Belg. – *Belgium*
Br., Brit. – *British, Britain*
Braz. – *Brazil*
C. – *Cape, (Cabo), Coast*
Can. – *Canada*
Cz. – *Czechoslovakia*
Den. – *Denmark*
Des. – *Desert*
Dist. – *District*
E. – *East*
Eng. – *England*
Fin. – *Finland*
Fr. – *France*
G. – *Gulf*
Ger. – *Germany*
Gr. – *Greece*
Gt. – *Great*
Hung. – *Hungary*
I.(s). – *Island)s((Isle, Ile)*
Indon. – *Indonesia*
Ire. – *Ireland*
It. – *Italy*
L. – *Lake, Lough, Loch, Lago*
Mex. – *Mexico*
Mor. – *Morocco*
Moz. – *Mozambique*
Mts. – *Mountains*
N. – *North, Northern*
Neth. – *Netherlands*
Nor. – *Norway*
N.Z. – *New Zealand*
Oc. – *Ocean*
Pac. – *Pacific*
Pen. – *Peninsula*
Phil. – *Philippines*
Pol. – *Poland*
Port. – *Portugal*
Pt. – *Point, Port*
R. – *River, Rio*
Reg. – *Region*
Rep. – *Republic*
Rum. – *Rumania*
S. – *Sea, South*
S. Afr. – *Rep. of South Africa*
Scot. – *Scotland*
st. – *state*
St. – *Saint*
Str. – *Strait*
Swed. – *Sweden*
Switz. – *Switzerland*
Terr. – *Territory*
Turk. – *Turkey*
U.K. – *United Kingdom*
U.S.A. – *United States of America*
U.S.S.R. – *Union of Soviet Socialist Republics*
Ven. – *Venezuela*
W. – *West*
Y-slav. – *Yugoslavia*

The bold figure indicates the map page. The latitudes and longitudes are intended primarily as a guide to finding the places on the map and in some cases are only approximate.

10 Aachen, Germany 50 47N 6 4E
30 Aba, Nigeria 5 10N 7 19E
21 Abadan, Iran 30 22N 48 20E
12 Abbeville, France 50 6N 1 50E
8 Aberdeen, Scotland 57 9N 2 6W
30 Abidjan, Ivory Coast 5 16N 3 58W
38 Acapulco 18 51N 99 56W
30 Accra, Ghana 5 35N 0 15W
9 Achill Hd., Ireland 53 59N 10 15W
21 Adana, Turkey 37 0N 35 16E
31 Addis Abeba, Ethiopia 9 2N 38 42E
27 Adelaide, Australia 34 55S 138 32E
21 Aden, South Yemen 12 50N 45 0E
21 Aden, G. of, Asia 12 0N 50 E
14 Adriatic Sea, Europe 43 0N 16 0E
15 Ægean Sea, Europe 37 0N 25 0E
21 Afghanistan, St. Asia 33 0N 65 0E
3 Africa, Continent 10 0N 20 0E
22 Agra, India 27 17N 78 13E
38 Aguascalientes, Mex. 22 0N 102 12W
22 Ahmadabad, India 23 0N 72 40E
12 Ajaccio, Corsica, Fr. 41 55N 8 40E
22 Ajmer, India 26 28N 74 37E
24 Akita, Japan 39 45N 140 0E
37 Akron, U.S.A. 41 7N 81 31W
18 Aktyubinsk, U.S.S.R. 50 20N 57 0E
16 Akureyri, Iceland 65 37N 18 3W
22 Akyab, Burma 20 15N 93 0E
21 Al Basrah, Iraq 30 30N 47 55E
21 Al Kuwayt, Kuwait 29 20N 48 0E
21 Al Madinah, Saudi Arabia 24 35N 39 52E
21 Al Mawsil, Iraq 34 0N 45 0E
39 Alajuela, Costa Rica 10 2N 84 8W
34 Alaska, st. U.S.A. 65 0N 150 0W
34 Alaska, G. of 58 0N 145 0W
13 Albacete, Spain 39 0N 1 50W
15 Albania, Rep., Europe 41 0N 20 0E
26 Albany, Australia 35 1S 117 58E
37 Albany, U.S.A. 42 40N 73 47W
17 Ålborg, Denmark 57 3N 9 52E
36 Albuquerque, U.S.A. 35 0N 106 40W
27 Albury, Australia 36 0S 146 50E
29 Aldabra Is., Indian Ocean 9 22S 46 28E
7 Alderney, I., Br. Isles 49 42N 2 12W
12 Alençon, France 48 27N 0 4E
14 Alessándria, Italy 44 54N 8 37E
16 Ålesund, Norway 62 28N 6 5E
34 Aleutian Is., Pac. Oc. 50 0N 175 0W
31 Alexandria = El Iskandarîya 31 0N 30 0E
30 Alger, Algeria 36 42N 3 8E
30 Algeria, St., N. Africa 32 50N 3 0E
13 Alicante, Spain 38 23N 0 30W
26 Alice Springs, Austral. 23 36S 133 53E
22 Allahabad, India 25 25N 81 58E
37 Allegheny Mts., U.S.A. 38 0N 80 0W
37 Allentown, U.S.A. 40 36N 75 30W
18 Alma Ata, U.S.S.R. 43 20N 76 50E
13 Almeria, Spain 36 52N 2 32W
10 Alps, Mts. Europe 46 30N 8 0E
24 Amagaskai, Japan 34 48N 135 35E
36 Amarillo, U.S.A. 35 14N 101 46W
41 Amazonas R., S. America 0 2S 53 30W
12 Amiens, France 49 54N 2 16E
20 Amirantes, Is., Indian Oc. 6 0S 53 0E
21 Amman, Jordan 32 0N 35 52E
22 Amritsar, India 31 35N 74 57E
10 Amsterdam, Neth. 52 23N 4 54E
34 Amundsen G., Canada 70 30N 123 0W
19 Amur, R., U.S.S.R. 53 30N 122 30E
34 Anchorage, Alaska 61 32N 149 50W
14 Ancona, Italy 43 37N 13 30E
22 Andaman Is., India 12 30N 92 30E
40 Andes Mts., 7 0S 85 0W
13 Andorra, st., Europe 42 30N 1 30E
14 Andria, Italy 41 13N 16 17E
39 Andros I., Bahama Is. 24 30N 78 0W
19 Angarsk, U.S.S.R. 52 30N 104 0E
12 Angers, France 47 30N 0 35W
6 Anglesey, I., Wales 53 17N 4 20W
33 Angola, st., Africa 12 0S 18 0E
12 Angoulême, France 45 39N 0 10E
21 Ankara, Turkey 40 0N 32 54E
30 Annaba, Algeria 36 55N 7 45E
25 Anshan, China 41 10N 123 0E
33 Antananarivo, Madagascar 18 55S 47 35E
39 Antigua, I., W. Indies 17 0N 61 50W
42 Antofagasta, Chile 23 50S 70 20W
9 Antrim, N. Ireland 54 40N 6 20W
25 Antung, China 40 10N 124 20E
10 Antwerpen, Belgium 51 13N 4 25E
24 Aomori, Japan 40 45N 140 45E
37 Appalachian Rs., U.S.A. 38 0N 80 0W
20 Arabian Sea, Asia 21 0N 63 0E
41 Aracajú, Brazil 11 0S 37 0W
23 Arafura Sea, E. Indies 10 0S 135 0E
41 Araguaia R., Brazil 7 0S 49 15W
22 Arakan Yoma, Burma 20 0N 94 30E
18 Aral Sea, U.S.S.R. 44 30N 60 0E
18 Aralsk, U.S.S.R. 46 50N 61 20E
8 Arbroath, Scotland 56 34N 2 35W
3 Arctic Ocean, Arctic 78 0N 160 0W
10 Ardennes, Belgium 49 30N 5 10E
39 Arecibo, Puerto Rico 18 29N 66 42W
17 Arendal, Norway 58 28N 8 46E
40 Arequipa, Peru 16 20S 71 30W
14 Arezzo, Italy 43 28N 11 50E
42 Argentina St., S. America 35 0S 60 0W
17 Arhus, Denmark 56 7N 10 11E
18 Arkhangelsk, U.S.S.R. 64 40N 41 0E
9 Arklow, Ireland 52 48N 6 10W
9 Armagh, N. Ireland 54 22N 6 40W
18 Armavir, U.S.S.R. 45 2N 41 7E
27 Armidale, Australia 30 36S 151 40E
10 Arnhem, Neth. 51 58N 5 55E
26 Arnhem Land, Australia 13 10S 135 0E
8 Arran, I., Scotland 55 34N 5 12W
12 Arras, France 50 17N 2 46E
17 Arvika, Sweden 59 42N 68 30E
29 Ascension, I., Atlantic Ocean 8 0S 14 15W
14 Ascoli Piceno, Italy 42 51N 13 34E
28 Ashburton, N.Z. 43 53S 171 48E
7 Ashford, England 51 8N 0 53E
18 Ashkhabad, U.S.S.R. 38 0N 57 50E
4 Asia, Continent 45 0N 75 0E
31 Asmera, Ethiopia 15 19N 38 55E
18 Astrakhan, U.S.S.R. 46 25N 48 5E
42 Asunción, Paraguay 25 11S 57 30W
31 Aswan, Egypt 24 4N 32 57E
31 Asyût, Egypt 27 11N 31 4E
42 Atacama, Desierto de, Chile 24 0S 69 20W
34 Athabasca, L., Canada 59 10N 109 30W
15 Athens = Athinai
15 Athinai, Greece 37 58N 23 46E
9 Athlone, Ireland 53 26N 7 57W
37 Atlanta, U.S.A. 33 50N 84 15W
2 Atlantic Ocean, 0 0 20 0W
28 Auckland, N.Z. 36 52S 174 46E
10 Augsburg, W. Germany 48 22N 10 54E
37 Augusta, U.S.A. 33 29N 81 59W
36 Austin, U.S.A. 30 20N 97 45W
26 Australia, Commonwealth of 10 35S to 43 38S 114 0E to 153 40E
27 Australian Alps, Austral. 36 30S 148 8E
10 Austria, st., Europe 47 0N 14 0E
42 Avellaneda, Argentina 34 50S 58 10W
12 Avignon, France 43 57N 4 50E
7 Avon, Co., England 51 26N 2 35W
7 Avon, R., England 52 8N 1 53W
7 Avonmouth, England 51 30N 2 42W
8 Ayr, Scotland 55 28N 4 37W
2 Azores, Is. Atlantic Oc. 38 44N 29 0W

B

41 Bacabal, Brazil 5 20S 56 45W
23 Bacolod, Philippines, 10 50N 123 0E
13 Badajoz, Spain 38 50N 6 59W
13 Badalona, Spain 41 26N 2 15E
35 Baffin B., Canada 72 0N 65 0W
35 Baffin I., Canada 68 0N 77 0W
21 Baghdad, Iraq 33 20N 44 30E
39 Bahamas, st., W. Indies 24 40N 74 0W
42 Bahía Blanca, Argentina 38 35S 62 13W
21 Bahrain, st., Asia 26 0N 50 35E
27 Bairnsdale, Australia 37 43S 147 35E
36 Bakersfield, U.S.A. 35 25N 119 0W
18 Baku, U.S.S.R. 40 25N 49 45E
13 Baleares, Islas, Spain 39 30N 3 0E
23 Bali, I., Indonesia 8 20S 115 0E
18 Balkhash, L., U.S.S.R. 46 0N 74 50E
27 Ballarat, Australia 37 33S 143 50E
9 Ballymena, N. Ireland 54 53N 6 18W
9 Ballymoney, N. Ireland 55 5N 6 30W
4 Baltic Sea, Europe 56 0N 20 0E
37 Baltimore, U.S.A. 39 18N 76 37W
30 Bamako, Mali 12 48N 7 59W
23 Banda Sea, Indonesia 6 0S 130 0E
* **23** Bandjarmasin, Indonesia 3 20S 114 25E
9 Bandon, Ireland 51 44N 8 45W
23 Bandung, Indonesia 6 36S 107 48E
39 Banes, Cuba 21 0N 75 42W
8 Banff, Scotland 57 40N 2 32W
22 Bangalore, India 12 59N 77 40E
31 Banghazi, Libya 32 11N 20 3E
23 Bangka, I., Indonesia 2 0S 105 50E
23 Bangkok = Krung Thep
22 Bangladesh, St., Asia 23 40N 90 0E
9 Bangor, N. Ireland 54 40N 5 40W
32 Bangui, Central Africa 4 23N 18 35E
34 Banks I., Canada 73 30N 120 0W
28 Banks Pen. N.Z. 43 45N 173 15E
9 Bantry, Ireland 51 40N 9 28W
39 Barahona, Dominican Rep. 18 13N 71 7W
18 Baranovichi, U.S.S.R. 53 10N 26 0E
39 Barbados, st., W. Indies 13 0N 59 30W
39 Barbuda, I., W. Indies 17 30N 61 40W
27 Barcaldine, Australia 23 33S 145 13E
13 Barcelona, Spain 41 21N 2 10E
22 Bareilly, India 28 22N 79 27E
18 Barents Sea, Arctic Oc. 73 0N 39 0E
14 Bari, Italy 41 6N 16 52E
14 Barletta, Italy 41 20N 16 17E
18 Barnaul, U.S.S.R. 53 20N 83 40E
6 Barnsley, England 53 33N 1 29W
† **22** Baroda, India 22 20N 73 10E
40 Barquisimeto, Ven. 9 58N 69 13W
8 Barra, I., Scotland 57 0N 7 30W
40 Barranquilla, Colombia 11 0N 74 50W
6 Barrow, England 54 8N 3 15W
10 Basel, Switzerland 47 35N 7 35E
7 Basildon, England 51 34N 0 29E
21 Basra = Al Basrah 30 30N 47 50E
27 Bass Str. Australia 40 0S 146 0E
22 Bassein, Burma 16 0N 94 30E
12 Bastia, Corsica, Fr. 42 40N 9 30E
7 Bath, England 51 22N 2 22W
27 Bathurst, Australia 33 25S 149 31E
37 Baton Rouge, U.S.A. 30 30N 91 5W
18 Batumi, U.S.S.R. 41 30N 41 30E
41 Bauru, Brazil 22 10S 49 0W
37 Bay City, U.S.A. 43 35N 83 51W
12 Bayeux, France 49 17N 0 42W
19 Baykal, L., U.S.S.R. 53 0N 108 0E
12 Bayonne, France 43 30N 1 28W
2 Beaufort Sea, 70 30N 146 0W
33 Beaufort West, S. Africa 32 18S 22 36E
37 Beaumont, U.S.A. 30 5N 94 8W
7 Bedford, & Co., England 52 8N 0 29W
33 Beira, Mozambique 19 50S 34 52E
21 Beirut, Lebanon 33 53N 35 31E
41 Belém, Brazil 1 20S 48 30W
9 Belfast, N. Ireland 54 35N 5 36W
12 Belfort, France 47 38N 6 50E
10 Belgium, King. Europe 51 30N 5 0E
18 Belgorod, U.S.S.R. 50 35N 36 35E
15 Belgrade = Beograd 44 50N 20 37E
38 Belize City, Bleize 17 25N 88 0W
38 Belize, st., Central America 17 0N 88 30W
2 Bellingshausen Sea, Antarctica 66 0S 80 0W
40 Bello, Colombia 6 20N 75 33W
41 Belo Horizonte, Brazil 20 0S 44 0W
8 Ben Nevis, Mt., Scot. 56 48N 5 0W
8 Benbecula, I., Scotland 57 26N 7 20W
27 Bendigo, Australia 36 40S 144 15E
22 Bengal, Gulf of, Asia 17 0N 89 0E
31 Benghazi = Banghazi 32 11N 20 3E
33 Benguela, Angola 12 37S 13 25E
30 Benin, st. (Dahomey) W. Africa 10 0N 2 0E
30 Benin City, Nigeria 6 20N 5 31E
33 Benoni, S. Africa 26 11S 28 18E
15 Beograd, (Belgrade) Yugoslavia 44 50N 20 37E
29 Berbera, Somali Rep. 10 30N 45 2E
18 Berezniki, U.S.S.R. 59 25N 56 5E
14 Bergamo, Italy 45 42N 9 40E
17 Bergen, Norwya 60 23N 5 27E
19 Bering Sea, U.S.S.R. 58 0N 167 0E
34 Bering Str. U.S.A./U.S.S.R. 66 0N 170 W
36 Berkeley, U.S.A. 38 0N 122 20W
7 Berkshire, Co., England 51 25N 1 0W
10 Berlin, Germany 52 32N 13 24E
10 Bern, Switzerland 46 57N 7 28E
6 Berwick-u.-Tweed, Eng. 55 47N 2 0W
12 Besançon, France 47 15N 6 0E
12 Béziers, France 43 20N 3 12E
22 Bhutan, St., Asia 27 25N 89 50E
11 Białystok, Poland 53 10N 23 10E
12 Biarritz, France 43 29N 1 33W
13 Bilbao, Spain 43 16N 2 56W
36 Billings, U.S.A. 45 43N 108 29W
6 Birkenhead, England 53 24N 3 1W
7 Birmingham, England 52 30N 1 55W
37 Birmingham, U.S.A. 33 40N 86 50W
9 Birr, Ireland 53 7N 7 55W
4 Biscay, B., Atlantic Oc. 45 0N 2 0W
15 Bitola, Yugoslavia 41 5N 21 21E
18 Biysk, U.S.S.R. 52 40N 85 0E
4 Black Sea, Europe 43 30N 35 0E
6 Blackburn, England 53 44N 2 30W
6 Blackpool, England 53 48N 3 3W
12 Blanc, Mont, France-Italy 45 48N 6 50E
33 Blantyre, Malawi 15 45S 35 0E
28 Blenheim, N.Z. 41 38S 174 5E
33 Bloemfontein, S. Africa 29 6S 26 14E
28 Bluff, N.Z. 46 37S 168 20E
30 Bobo Dioulasso, Upper Volta 11 8N 4 13W
16 Boden, Sweden 65 50N 21 42E
16 Bodø, Norway 67 17N 14 27E
40 Bogotá, Colombia 4 34N 74 0W
40 Bolivia, St., S. America 17 6S 64 0W
14 Bologna, Italy 44 30N 11 20E
6 Bolton, England 53 35N 2 26W
14 Bolzano, Italy 46 30N 11 20E
22 Bombay, India 18 55N 72 50E
32 Boma, Zaïre 5 50S 13 4E
35 Bonavista, Canada 48 40N 53 5W
10 Bonn, W. Germany 50 43N 7 6E
6 Bootle, England 53 28N 3 1W
17 Borås, Sweden 57 42N 13 1E
12 Bordeaux, France 44 50N 0 36W
8 Borders, Co. Scotland 55 30N 3 0W
17 Borlange, Sweden 60 28N 15 25E
23 Borneo, I. E. Indies 1 0N 115 0E
17 Bornholm, I., Denmark 55 8N 14 55E
15 Bosna, R., Yugoslavia 44 50N 18 10E
37 Boston, U.S.A. 42 20N 71 0W
16 Bothnia, G. of, Europe 63 0N 21 0E
33 Botswana, st. Africa 23 0S 24 0E
42 Botucatu, Brazil 22 55S 48 30W
30 Bouaké, Ivory Coast 7 40N 4 55W
12 Boulogne, France 50 42N 1 36E
12 Bourges, France 47 5N 2 22E
27 Bourke, Australia 30 8S 145 55E
7 Bournemouth, England 50 43N 1 53W
27 Bowen, Australia 20 0S 148 16E
9 Boyle, Ireland 53 58N 8 19W
6 Bradford, England 53 47N 1 45W
13 Braga, Portugal 41 35N 8 32W
22 Brahmaputra, R., India 26 30N 93 30E
34 Brandon, Canada 49 50N 100 0W
35 Brantford, Canada 43 15N 80 15W
41 Brasília, Brazil 15 30S 47 30W
11 Brasov, Rumania 45 7N 25 39E
10 Bratislava, Cz. 48 10N 17 7E
10 Braunschweig, W.Ger. 52 17N 10 28E
41 Brazil, St., S. America 5 0N to 34 0S 35 0W to 74 0W
32 Brazzaville, Congo 4 9S 15 12E
10 Bremen, W. Germany 53 4N 8 47E
10 Bremerhaven, W.Ger. 53 34N 8 35E
14 Bréscia, Italy 45 33N 10 13E
12 Brest, France 48 24N 4 31W
37 Bridgeport, U.S.A. 41 12N 73 12W
39 Bridgetown, Barbados 13 0N 59 30W
7 Brighton, England 50 50N 0 9W
15 Bríndisi, Italy 40 39N 17 55E
27 Brisbane, Australia 27 25S 152 54E
7 Bristol, England 51 26N 2 35W
7 Bristol, Chan., U.K. 51 18N 3 30W
2 British Antarctic Terr., Antarctica 67 0S 40 0W
3 British Indian Ocean Terr. Indian Ocean 5 0S 70 0E
10 Brno, Czechoslovakia 49 10N 16 35E
15 Brod, Yugoslavia 41 35N 21 17E
8 Brodick, Scotland 55 34N 5 9W
27 Broken Hill, Australia 31 58S 141 29E
10 Brugge, Belgium 51 13N 3 13E
23 Brunei, st. Asia 4 50N 115 0E
10 Brussel, Belgium 50 51N 4 21E
18 Bryansk, U.S.S.R. 53 15N 34 20E
40 Bucaramanga, Colombia 7 0N 73 0W
11 Bucharest = Bucureşti 44 27N 26 10E
7 Buckinghamshire, Co., England 52 0N 0 59W
11 Bucureşti, Rumania 44 27N 26 10E
11 Budapest, Hungary 47 29N 19 5E
42 Buenos Aires, Arg. 34 30S 58 20W
37 Buffalo, U.S.A. 42 55N 78 50W
33 Bulawayo, Rhodesia 20 7S 28 32E
15 Bulgaria St. Europe 42 35N 34 30E
26 Bunbury, Australia 33 20S 115 35E
27 Bundaberg, Australia 24 54S 152 22E
9 Bundoran, Ireland 54 24N 8 17W
24 Bungō-Suidō, Japan 33 0N 132 15E
31 Bûr Said, Egypt 31 16N 32 18E
31 Bûr Sûdan, Egypt 19 32N 37 9E
15 Burgas, Bulgaria 42 33N 27 29E
13 Burgos, Spain 42 21N 3 42W
22 Burma, St., Asia 21 0N 96 30E
27 Burnie, Australia 41 4S 145 56E
6 Burnley, England 53 47N 2 15W
21 Bursa, Turkey 40 15N 29 5E
6 Burton-on-Trent, England 52 48N 1 39W
32 Burundi, st., Africa 3 0S 30 0E
6 Bury, England 53 47N 2 15W
21 Bushehr, Iran 28 55N 50 55E
36 Butte, U.S.A. 46 0N 112 31W
11 Bydgoszcz, Poland 53 10N 18 0E

C

32 Cabinda, Reg., Angola 5 40S 12 11E
13 Cáceres, Spain 39 26N 6 23W
13 Cádiz, Spain 36 30N 6 20W
12 Caen, France 49 10N 0 22W
6 Caernarfon, Wales 53 8N 4 17W
14 Cágliari, Sardinia, Italy 39 15N 9 6E
39 Caguas, Puerto Rico 18 14N 66 4W
39 Caicos Is., W. Indies 21 40N 71 40W
8 Cairngorm, Mts., Scot. 57 6N 3 42W
27 Cairns, Australia 16 55S 145 51E
31 Cairo = El Qahira 30 1N 31 14E
12 Calais, France 50 57N 1 56E
22 Calcutta, India 22 36N 88 24E
34 Calgary, Canada 51 0N 114 10W
40 Cali, Colombia 3 25N 76 35W
22 Calicut, India 11 15N 75 43E
38 California, G. of, Mex. 27 0N 111 0W
40 Callao, Peru 12 0S 77 0W
14 Caltanissetta, Sicily, Italy 37 30N 14 3E
39 Camagüey, Cuba 21 20N 78 0W
23 Cambodia 13 0N 105 0E
7 Camborne, England 50 13N 5 18W
7 Cambrian, Mts., Wales 52 10N 3 52W
7 Cambridge, & Co., Eng. 52 13N 0 8E
32 Cameroon, st., Africa 5 0N 12 30E
38 Campeche, B. de, Mex. 19 30N 93 0W
41 Campina Grande, Brazil 17 20S 35 37W
42 Campinas, Brazil 22 50S 47 0W
41 Campo Grande, Brazil 20 25S 54 40W
41 Campos, Brazil 21 50S 41 20W
34 Canada, st., N.America 60 0N 100 0W
38 Canal Zone, Panama 9 0N 79 45W
30 Canary Is. (Canarias Isles) Atlantic Oc. 29 30N 17 0W
27 Canberra, Australia 35 15S 149 8E
12 Cannes, France 43 32N 7 0E
7 Canterbury, England 51 17N 1 5E
28 Canterbury Bight, N.Z. 44 16S 171 55E
28 Canterbury Plains, N.Z. 43 55S 171 22E
37 Canton, China 23 15N 113 15E
39 Cap Haïtien, Haiti 19 40N 72 20W
35 Cape Breton I., Canada 46 0N 61 0W
33 Cape Town, S. Africa 33 56S 18 28E
2 Cape Verde Is., Atlantic Oc. 17 10N 25 20W
27 Cape York Pen. Australia 13 30S 142 30E
40 Caracas, Venezuela 10 30N 66 50W
7 Cardiff, Wales 51 28N 3 11W
7 Cardigan, B., Wales 52 30N 4 30W
39 Caribbean Sea, W. Indies 15 0N 75 0W
6 Carlisle, England 54 54N 2 55W
9 Carlow, & Co., Ireland 52 50N 6 58W
7 Carmarthen, Wales 51 56N 4 8W
26 Carnarvon, Australia 24 51S 113 42E
3 Caroline Is., Pacific Oc. 8 0N 150 0E
11 Carpathians, Mts. Europe 46 20N 26 0E
27 Carpentaria, G. of, Austral. 14 0S 139 0E
13 Cartagena, Colombia 10 20N 75 30W
40 Cartagena, Spain 37 38N 0 59W
41 Caruaru, Brazil 8 15S 35 55W
40 Carúpano, Venezuela 10 45N 63 15W
30 Casablanca, Morocco 33 30N 7 37W
36 Casper, U.S.A. 42 52N 106 27W
18 Caspian Sea, U.S.S.R. 43 0N 50 0E
13 Castellón de la Plana, Spain 39 58N 0 3W
9 Castlebar, Ireland 53 52N 9 20W
9 Castlereagh, Ireland 53 47N 8 30W
39 Castries, W. Indies 14 0N 60 50W
14 Catánia, Sicily, Italy 37 31N 15 4E
14 Catanzaro, Italy 38 53N 16 36E
9 Cavan & Co., Ireland 54 0N 7 22W
41 Cayenne, Fr. Guiana 5 0N 52 18W
39 Cayman Is., W. Indies 19 40N 79 50W
23 Cebu, Philippes 10 30N 124 0E
37 Cedar Rapids, U.S.A. 42 0N 91 38W
23 Celebes, I. (Sulawesi) Indonesia 2 0S 120 0E
23 Celebes Sea, Asia 3 0N 123 0E
8 Central, Co. Scotland 56 20N 4 20W
32 Central Africa, st., Africa 7 0N 20 0E
23 Ceram Sea, Indonesia 2 30S 128 30E
30 Ceuta, Morocco 25 52N 5 26W
22 Ceylon = Sri Lanka
31 Chad. st., Africa 12 0N 17 0E
3 Chagos Arch., Indian Oc. 6 0S 72 0E
12 Châlon, France 46 48N 4 50E
12 Châlons, France, 48 48N 4 20E
12 Chambéry, France 45 34N 5 55E
25 Changchow, China 31 45N 120 0E
25 Changchun, China 43 58N 125 9E
25 Changkiakow, China 40 52N 114 45E
25 Changkiang, China 21 7N 110 21E
25 Changsha, China 28 5N 113 1E
7 Channel Is., British Is. 49 30N 2 40W
37 Charleston, U.S.A. 32 55N 80 0W
27 Charleville, Australia 26 24S 146 15E
37 Charlotte, U.S.A. 35 16N 80 46W
37 Charlottesville, U.S.A. 38 1N 78 30W
35 Charlottetown, Canada 46 19N 63 3W
27 Charters Towers, Australia 20 5S 146 13E
12 Chartres, France 48 29N 1 30E
35 Chatham, Canada 47 2N 65 28W
37 Chattanooga, U.S.A. 35 0N 85 20W
18 Cheboksary, U.S.S.R. 56 8N 47 30E
7 Chelmsford, England 51 44N 0 29E
7 Cheltenham, England 51 53N 2 7W
18 Chelyabinsk, U.S.S.R. 55 10N 61 35E
25 Chengchow, China 34 45N 113 45E
25 Chengtu, China 30 40N 104 12E
12 Cherbourg, France 49 39N 1 40W
18 Cherepovets, U.S.S.R. 59 5N 37 55E
18 Chernigov, U.S.S.R. 51 28N 31 20E
18 Chernovtsy, U.S.S.R. 48 0N 26 0E
7 Cherwell, R., England 51 56N 1 18W
37 Chesapeake B., U.S.A. 38 0N 76 12W
6 Cheshire, Co., England 53 14N 2 30W
6 Chester, England 53 12N 2 53W
6 Chesterfield, England 53 14N 1 26W
36 Cheyenne, U.S.A. 41 9N 104 49W
24 Chiba, Japan 35 30N 140 7E
37 Chicago, U.S.A. 41 56N 87 50W
40 Chidayo, Peru 6 42S 79 50W
35 Chicoutimi, Canada 48 28N 71 5W
38 Chihuahua, Mexico 28 40N 106 3W
42 Chile St., S. America 17 30S to 55 0S 71 15W
42 Chillán, Chile 36 40S 72 10W
7 Chiltern Hills, England 51 44N 0 42W
40 Chimbote, Peru 9 0S 78 35W
18 Chimkent, U.S.S.R. 42 40N 69 25E
25 China, st., Asia 55 0N to 18 30W 70 0E to 133 0E
39 Chinandego, Nicaragua 12 30N 87 0W
25 Chinchow, China 41 10N 121 10E
19 Chita, U.S.S.R. 52 0N 113 25E
22 Chittagong, Bangladesh 22 19N 91 55E
25 Chongjin, N. Korea 41 40N 129 40E
11 Chorzów, Poland 50 18N 19 0E
28 Christchurch, N.Z. 43 33S 172 39E
24 Chūgaku-Sanchi, Japan 35 0N 133 0E
25 Chungking, China 29 35N 106 50E
34 Churchill, Canada 58 45N 94 5W
39 Ciego de Avila, Cuba 21 50N 78 50W
39 Cienfuegos, Cuba 22 10N 80 30W
37 Cincinnati, U.S.A. 39 8N 84 25W
38 Ciudad Acuña, Mex. 29 20N 101 10W
38 Ciudad Juárez, Mex. 31 40N 106 28W
38 Ciudad Madero, Mex. 22 19N 97 50W

* *Renamed Banjarmasin*
† *Renamed Vadodara*

38 Ciudad Obregón, Mexico 27 28N 109 59W
13 Ciudad Real, Spain 38 59N 3 55W
38 Ciudad Victoria, Mex. 23 41N 99 9W
9 Clare, Co., Ireland 52 52N 8 35W
9 Claremorris, Ireland 53 45N 9 0W
27 Clermont, Australia 22 46S 147 38E
12 Clermont Ferrand, France 45 46N 3 4E
37 Cleveland, U.S.A. 41 28N 81 43W
6 Cleveland, Co., England 54 35N 1 20W
27 Cloncurry, Australia 20 40S 140 28E
9 Clones, Ireland 54 10N 7 13W
11 Cluj, Rumania 46 47N 23 38E
6 Clwyd, Co., Wales 53 10N 3 30W
8 Clyde, Firth of, Scotland 55 20N 5 0W
8 Clyde, R., Scotland 55 46N 3 58W
8 Clydebank, Scotland 55 54N 4 25W
36 Coast Ra., N. America 40 0N 124 0W
8 Coatbridge, Scotland 55 52N 4 2W
38 Coatzacoalcos, Mexico 18 7N 94 35W
35 Cobalt, Canada 47 25N 79 42W
9 Cobh, Ireland 51 50N 8 18W
40 Cochabamba, Bolivia 17 15S 66 20W
35 Cochrane, Canada 49 0N 81 0W
3 Cocos Is., Indian Oc. 12 12S 96 54E
22 Coimbatore, India 11 2N 76 59E
13 Coimbra, Portugal 40 15N 8 27W
7 Colchester, England 51 54N
9 Coleraine, N. Ireland 55 8N 6 40E
38 Colima, Mexico 19 10N 103 40W
8 Coll, I., Scotland 56 40N 6 3W
9 Collooney, Ireland 54 11N 8 28W
10 Cologne = Köln, W.Ger. 50 56N 8 58E
40 Colombia, St., S. America 3 45N 73 0W
22 Colombo, Sri Lanka 6 56N 79 58E
38 Colon, Panama 9 20N 80 0W
8 Colonsay, I., Scotland 56 4N 6 12W
36 Colorado, R., U.S.A. 33 30N 114 30W
36 Colorado Springs, U.S.A. 38 50N 104 50W
37 Columbia, U.S.A. 34 0N 81 0W
36 Columbia, R., U.S.A. 51 50N 118 0W
37 Columbus, Ga., U.S.A. 32 30N 84 58W
37 Columbus, Ohio, U.S.A. 39 57N 83 1W
6 Colwyn Bay, Wales 53 17N 3 44W
14 Como, Italy 45 48N 9 5E
30 Conakry, Guinea 9 29N 13 49W
42 Concepción, Chile 36 50S 73 0W
42 Concepción, Paraguay 23 30S 57 20W
42 Concordia, Argentina 31 20S 58 2W
32 Congo, R., Africa 2 0N 23 0E
32 Congo, st., Africa 2 0S 16 0E
11 Constanţa, Rumania 44 14N 28 38E
30 Constantine, Algeria 36 25N 6 30E
28 Cook Is., Pacific Oc. 22 0S 157 0W
28 Cook, Mt., N.Z. 43 36S 170 9E
28 Cook Str., N.Z. 41 15S 174 29E
27 Cooktown, Australia 15 30S 145 16E
26 Coolgardie, Australia 30 55S 121 8E
17 Copenhagen = København
27 Coral Sea Is., Terr., 20 0S 155 0E
42 Córdoba, Argentina 31 20S 64 10W
13 Córdoba, Spain 37 50N 4 50W
15 Corfu = Kérkira, I.
9 Cork, & Co., Ireland 51 54N 8 30W
35 Corner Brook, Canada 49 0N 58 0W
7 Cornwall, Co., England 50 26N 4 40W
36 Corpus Christi, U.S.A. 27 50N 97 28W
42 Corrientes, Argentina 27 30S 58 45W
12 Corsica, I. Mediterranean Sea 42 0N 9 0E
14 Cosenza, Italy 39 17N 16 14E
39 Costa Rica st., Central America 10 0N 84 0W
30 Cotonou, Benin 6 20N 2 25E
7 Cotswold Hills, England 51 42N 2 10W
7 Coventry, England 52 25N 1 31W
27 Cowra, Australia 33 49S 148 42E
11 Craiova, Rumania 44 21N 23 48E
14 Cremona, Italy 45 8N 10 2E
15 Crete = Kriti, I. 35 20N 25 0E
6 Crewe, England 53 6N 2 28W
39 Cuba, st., W. Indies 22 0N 79 0W
40 Cúcuta, Colombia 8 0N 72 30W
40 Cuenca, Ecuador 2 50S 79 9W
13 Cuenca, Spain 45 0N 2 10W
41 Cuiabá, Brazil 15 30S 56 0W
38 Culiacan, Mexico 24 50N 107 40W
6 Cumbria, Co., England 54 30N 3 0W
6 Cumbrian, Mts., Eng. 54 30N 3 0W
27 Cunnamulla, Australia 28 2S 145 38E
40 Curaçao, Neth. W. Indies 12 10N 69 0W
40 Curaray, R., Peru 1 30S 75 30W
42 Curitiba, Brazil 25 20S 49 10W
21 Cyprus, st., Medit. Sea 35 0N 33 0E
10 Czechoslovakia, st. Europe 49 0N 17 0E
11 Czestochowa, Poland 50 49N 19 7E

D

23 Da Nang, Vietnam 16 10N 108 7E
22 Dacca, Bangladesh 23 43N 90 26E
30 Dahomey = Benin
30 Dakar, Senegal 14 34N 17 29W
27 Dalby, Australia 27 10S 151 17E
37 Dallas, U.S.A. 32 50N 96 50W
21 Damascus = Dimashq
26 Dampier, Australia 20 40S 116 30E
28 Dannevirke, N.Z. 40 12S 176 8E
11 Danube, R., Europe 45 0N 28 20E
32 Dar-es-Salaam, Tanzania 6 50S 39 12E
28 Dargaville, N.Z. 35 57S 173 52E
40 Darien, G. del, Colombia 9 0N 77 0W
27 Darling, R., Austral. 31 0S 144 30E
26 Darling Ra., Australia 32 30S 116 0E
6 Darlington, England 54 33N 1 33W
7 Dartmoor, England 50 36N 4 0W
35 Dartmouth, Canada 44 40N 63 30W
26 Darwin, Austral. 12 20S 130 50E
18 Daugavpils, U.S.S.R. 55 53N 26 32E
34 Dauphin, Canada 51 15N 100 5W
23 Davao, Philippines 7 0N 125 40E
39 David, Panama 8 30N 82 30W
35 Davis Str., N. America 66 30N 59 0W
34 Dawson, Canada 64 10N 139 30W
34 Dawson Creek, Can. 55 45N 120 15W
37 Dayton, U.S.A. 39 45N 84 10W
11 Debrecen, Hungary 47 33N 21 42E
8 Dee, R., Scotland 57 4N 3 7W
22 Delhi, India 28 38N 77 17E
17 Denmark, st., Europe 55 30N 9 0E
2 Denmark Str., Atlantic Oc. 66 0N 30 0W
36 Denver, U.S.A. 39 48N 105 0W
26 Derby, Australia 17 18S 123 40E
6 Derby & Co., England 52 55N 1 28W
37 Des Moines, U.S.A. 41 29N 93 40W
37 Detroit, U.S.A. 42 20N 83 5W
7 Devon, Co., England 50 45N 3 45W
28 Devonport, N.Z. 36 49S 174 49E
6 Dewsbury, England 53 42N 1 38W
* 33 Diego-Suarez, Madagascar 12 25S 49 20E
12 Dieppe, France 49 54N 1 4E
12 Dijon, France 47 20N 5 0E
21 Dimashq (Damasus) Syria 33 30N 36 18E
8 Dingwall, Scotland 57 36N 4 26W
23 Djakarta, Indonesia 6 9S 106 49E
29 Djibouti, st., Africa 11 30N 43 3E
18 Dnepropetrovsk, U.S.S.R. 48 30N 35 0E
39 Dominica, I., Winward Is. 15 20N 61 20W
39 Dominican Republic, st. W. Indies 19 0N 70 30W
8 Don, R., Scotland 57 14N 2 15W
6 Doncaster, England 53 31N 1 9W
9 Donegal & Co., Ireland 54 39N 8 8W
9 Donegal, B., Ireland 54 30N 8 35W
18 Donetsk, U.S.S.R. 48 7N 37 50E
7 Dorset, Co., England 50 48N 2 25W
10 Dortmund, W. Germany 51 32N 7 28E
12 Douai, France 50 21N 3 4E
32 Douala, Cameroon 4 0N 9 45E
6 Douglas, I. of Man 54 9N 4 29W
13 Douro, R., Portugal 41 1N 8 16W
7 Dover, England 51 7N 1 19E
33 Drakensberg, Mts., S. Africa 31 0S 25 0E
17 Drammen, Norway 59 42N 10 12E
15 Drava, R., Yugoslavia 45 50N 18 0W
10 Dresden, E. Germany 51 2N 13 45E
15 Drina, R., Yugoslavia 44 30N 19 10E
9 Drogheda, Ireland 53 45N 6 20W
34 Drumheller, Canada 51 25N 112 40W
27 Dubbo, Australia 32 11S 148 35E
9 Dublin & Co., Ireland 53 20N 6 18W
15 Dubrovnik, Y-slav. 42 39N 18 6E
10 Duisburg, W. Germany 51 27N 6 42E
37 Duluth, U.S.A. 46 48N 92 10W
8 Dumbarton, Scotland 55 58N 4 35W
8 Dumfries, Scotland 55 12N 3 30W
8 Dumfries & Galloway, Co., Scot. 55 10N 3 50W
9 Dun Lagohaire, Ierland 53 17N 6 9W
9 Dundalk, Ireland 53 55N 6 45W
8 Dundee, Scotland 56 29N 3 0W
28 Dunedin, N.Z. 45 50S 170 33E
8 Dunfermline, Scotland 56 5N 3 28W
9 Dungannon, N. Ireland 54 30N 6 47W
9 Dungarvan, Ireland 52 6N 7 40W
12 Dunkerque, France 51 2N 2 20E
8 Dunnet Hd., Scotland 58 38N 3 22W
38 Durango, U.S.A. 37 10N 107 50W
33 Durban, S. Africa 29 49S 31 1E
6 Durham, Co., England 54 42N 1 45W
18 Dushanbe, U.S.S.R. 38 50N 68 50E
10 Düsseldorf, W.Ger. 51 15N 6 46E
7 Dyfed, Co., Wales 52 0N 4 0W
18 Dzerzhinsk, U.S.S.R. 56 15N 43 15E
25 Dzungaria, China 44 10N 88 0E

E

25 East China Sea, Asia 27 0N 125 0E
33 East London, S. Africa 33 0S 27 55E
7 East Sussex, Co., England 51 0N 0 30E
7 Eastbourne, England 50 46N 0 18E
22 Eastern Ghats, India 15 0N 80 0E
13 Ebro, R., Spain 41 49N 1 5W
40 Ecuador, St., S. America 22 0S 79 0W
8 Edinburgh, Scotland 55 57N 3 12W
34 Edmonton, Canada 53 30N 113 30W
35 Edmundston, Canada 47 23N 68 20W
31 Egypt, st., N. Africa 25 0N 30 0E
10 Eindhoven, Netherlands 51 26N 5 30E
31 El Faiyûm, Egypt 29 19N 30 50E
13 El Ferrol, Spain 43 29N 3 14W
31 El Gîza, Egypt 30 0N 31 10E
31 El Iskandarîya, (Alexandria) Egypt 31 0N 30 0E
31 El Khartûm, Sudan 15 31N 32 35E
31 El Marsûra, Egypt 31 0N 31 19E
31 El Minyâ, Egypt 28 7N 30 33E
31 El Obeid, Sudan 13 8N 30 10E
36 El Paso, U.S.A. 31 50N 106 30W
31 El Qâhira (Cairo) Egypt 30 1N 31 14E
31 El Suweis (Suez) Egypt 29 58N 32 31E
14 Elba, I., Italy 42 48N 10 15E
10 Elbe, R. Germany 53 15N 10 7E
18 Elbrus, Mt., U.S.S.R. 43 30N 42 30E
21 Elburz Mts., Iran 36 0N 52 0E
13 Elche, Spain 38 15N 0 42W
8 Elgin, Scotland 57 39N 3 20W
2 Ellesmere I., Canada 79 30N 80 0W
3 Ellice Is. (Tuvalu), Pacific Oc. 8 0S 176 0E
27 Emerald, Australia 23 30S 148 11E
38 Empalme, Mexico 28 1N 110 49W
3 Enderby Land, Antarctica 66 0S 53 0E
18 Engels, U.S.S.R. 51 28N 46 6E
6 England, U.K. 50 to 55 45N 1 40E to 5 40W
7 English Chan., Europe 50 0N 2 0W
9 Ennis, Ireland 52 51N 8 59W
9 Enniskillen, N. Ireland 52 30N 6 35W
32 Entebbe, Uganda 0 3N 32 30E
30 Enugu, Nigeria 6 30N 7 30E
32 Equatorial Guinea, st., Africa 2 0N 10 E
37 Erie, U.S.A. 42 7N 80 2W
37 Erie, L., N. America 42 30N 82 0W
31 Eritrea, Reg., Ethiopia 14 0N 41 0E

* *Renamed Antseranana*

9 Erne, L., N. Ireland 54 14N 7 30W
21 Erzurum, Turkey 39 57N 41 15E
17 Esbjerg, Denmark 55 29N 8 29E
21 Esfahan, Iran 32 43N 51 33E
17 Eskilstuna, Sweden 59 22N 16 32E
26 Esperance, Australia 33 45S 121 55E
40 Essequibo, R., Guyana 5 45N 58 50W
10 Essen, W. Germany 51 28N 6 59E
7 Essex, Co., England 51 48N 0 30E
31 Ethiopia, st., Africa 8 0N 40 0E
14 Etna, Mt., Italy 37 45N 15 0E
36 Eugene, U.S.A. 44 0N 123 8W
21 Euphrates, R., Iraq 33 30N 43 0E
37 Evansville, U.S.A. 38 0N 87 35W
22 Everest, Mt., Nepal 28 5N 86 58E
15 Evvoia, I., Greece 38 30N 24 0E
7 Exeter, England 50 43N 3 31W
27 Eyre, L., Australia 29 0S 137 20E
26 Eyre Pen., Australia 33 30S 137 17E

F

17 Fagersta, Sweden 60 1N 15 46E
34 Fairbanks, Alaska 64 59N 147 40W
8 Falkirk, Scotland 56 0N 3 47W
42 Falkirk Islands, Atlantic Oc. 51 30S 58 30W
2 Falkland Islands Dependencies, Southern Oc. 55 0S 45 0W
17 Falun, Sweden 60 32N 15 39E
7 Fareham, England 50 52N 1 11W
37 Fargo, U.S.A. 47 0N 97 0W
2 Faroe Is., N. Atlantic Oc. 62 0N 7 0W
28 Fielding, N.Z. 40 13S 175 35E
7 Felixtowe, England 51 58N 1 22W
14 Ferrard, Italy 44 50N 11 26E
30 Fés, Morocco 34 5N 4 54W
8 Fife, Co., Scotland 56 13N 3 2W
28 Fiji, Is., Pacific Ocean 17 20S 179 0E
8 Findhorn, R., Scotland 57 30N 3 45W
13 Finisterre, C., Spain 42 50N 9 19W
16 Finland, st., Europe 70 0N 27 0E
14 Firenze, Italy 43 47N 11 15E
7 Fishguard, Wales 51 59N 4 59W
6 Flamborough Hd., Eng. 54 8N 0 4W
10 Flensburg, Germany 54 46N 9 28E
27 Flinders Ra., Australia 31 30S 138 30E
37 Flint, U.S.A. 43 0N 83 40W
23 Flores Sea, Indonesia 6 30S 124 0E
14 Florence = Firenze
42 Florianópolis, Brazil 27 30S 48 30W
37 Florida Str., U.S.A. 25 0N 80 0W
14 Fóggia, Italy 41 28N 15 31E
7 Folkestone, England 51 5N 1 11E
12 Fontainbleau, France 48 24N 2 40E
25 Foochow, China 26 9N 119 25E
25 Formosa = Taiwan
4 Føroyar, Is., Atlantic Oc. 62 0N 7 0W
37 Fort Smith, U.S.A. 35 25N 94 25W
37 Fort Wayne, U.S.A. 41 5N 85 10W
8 Fort William, Scotland 56 48N 5 8W
36 Fort Worth, U.S.A. 32 45N 97 25W
34 Fort Yukon, Alaska 66 35N 145 12W
39 Fort-de-France, Martinique 14 36N 61 2W
41 Fortaleza, Brazil 3 35S 38 35W
8 Forth, Firth of, Scotland 56 5N 2 55W
12 France, st., Europe 47 0N 3 0E
10 Frankfurt, W. Germany 50 7N 8 40E
34 Fraser, R., Canada 53 30N 120 40W
8 Fraserburgh, Scotland 57 41N 2 0W
35 Fredericton, Canada 45 57N 66 40W
17 Frederikshavn, Den. 57 28N 10 31E
17 Fredrikstad, Norway 59 13N 10 57E
39 Freeport, Bahamas 42 18N 89 40W
30 Freetown, Sierra Leone 8 30N 13 10W
10 Freiburg, Germany 48 0N 7 52E
26 Fremantle, Australia 32 1S 115 47E
41 French Guiana, S. America 4 0N 53 0W
38 Fresnillo, Mexico 23 10N 103 0W
36 Fresno, U.S.A. 36 47N 119 50W
18 Frunze, U.S.S.R. 42 40N 74 50E
24 Fukuoka, Japan 33 30N 130 30E
24 Funabashi, Japan 33 45N 140 0E
27 Furneaux Group, Is., Tasmania 40 10S 147 56E
25 Fushun, China 41 55N 123 55E
17 Fyn, I., Denmark 55 18N 10 20E
8 Fyne, L., Denmark 55 20N 10 30E

G

32 Gabon, st., Africa 2 0S 12 0E
15 Gabrovo, Bulgaria 42 52N 25 27E
2 Galapagos Is., Pacific Oc. 0 0 89 0W
11 Galaţi, Rumania 45 27N 28 2E
16 Gällivare, Sweden 67 7N 20 32E
8 Galloway, Mull of, Scot. 54 38N 4 50W
37 Galveston, U.S.A. 29 15N 94 48W
9 Galway & Co., Ireland 53 16N 9 4W
9 Galway, B., Ireland 53 10N 9 20W
30 Gambia, st., W. Africa 13 25N 16 0W
22 Ganga, R., India 25 0N 88 0E
22 Ganges, R. = Ganga R.
14 Garda, L. di, Italy 45 40N 10 40E
12 Garonne, R., France 44 45N 0 32W
35 Gaspé Pen., Canada 48 45N 65 40W
6 Gateshead, England 54 57N 1 37W
17 Gävle, Sweden 60 41N 17 13E
31 Gaza, Egypt 31 30N 34 28E
11 Gdańsk, Poland 54 22N 18 40E
11 Gdyñia, Poland 54 35N 18 33E
27 Geelong, Australia 38 2S 144 20E
10 Genève, Switzerland 46 12N 6 9E
14 Génova (Genoa) Italy 44 24N 8 56E
10 Gent, Belgium 51 2N 3 37E
40 Georgetown, Guyana 6 50N 58 12W
26 Geraldton, Australia 28 48S 114 32E
10 Germany, East, st. Europe 52 0N 12 0E
10 Germany, West, st., Europe 52 0N 9 0E
33 Germiston, S. Africa 26 11S 28 10E
13 Gerona, Spain 41 58N 2 46E
30 Ghana, st., W. Africa 6 0N 1 0W
9 Giant's Causeway, N. Ireland 55 15N 6 30W
13 Gibraltar, Europe 36 7N 5 22W
26 Gibson Desert, Australia 24 0S 125 0E
24 Gifu, Japan 35 30N 136 45E
13 Gijón, Spain 43 32N 5 42W
* 3 Gilbert Is., Pacific Oc. 1 0S 176 0E
7 Gillingham, England 51 23N 0 34E
8 Girvan, Scotland 55 15N 4 50W
28 Gisborne, N.Z. 38 39S 178 5E
17 Gjøvik, Norway 60 47N 10 43E
35 Glace Bay, Canada 46 11N 59 58W
27 Gladstone, Australia 23 52S 151 16E
17 Glamå, R., Norway 60 30N 12 8E
8 Glasgow, Scotland 55 52N 4 14W
27 Glen Innes, Australia 29 40S 151 39E
36 Glendale, U.S.A. 34 7N 118 18W
7 Gloucester & Co., England 51 52N 2 15W
22 Godavari, R., India 19 5N 79 0E
41 Goiânia, Brazil 16 35S 49 20W
18 Gomel, U.S.S.R. 52 28N 31 0E
38 Gómez Palacio, Mexico 25 40N 104 40W
33 Good Hope, C. of, S. Africa 34 24S 18 30E
28 Gore, N.Z. 46 5S 168 58E
18 Gorkiy, U.S.S.R. 57 20N 44 0E
7 Gosport, England 50 48N 1 8W
17 Göteborg, Sweden 57 43N 11 59E
17 Gotland, I., Swdeen 58 15N 18 30E
27 Goulburn, Australia 32 22S 149 31E
41 Governador Valadares, Brazil 18 15S 41 57W
14 Gozo, I., Malta 36 0N 14 13E
27 Grafton, Australia 29 35S 152 0E
2 Graham Land, Antacrtica 67 0S 65 0W
33 Grahamstown, S. Africa 33 19S 26 31E
8 Grampian, Co., Scot. 57 30N 2 40W
8 Grampian Highlands, Scotland 56 50N 4 0W
39 Granada, Nicaragua 11 58N 86 0W
13 Granada, Spain 37 10N 3 35W
36 Grand Canyon, U.S.A. 36 20N 113 30W
37 Grand Forks, U.S.A. 48 0N 97 3W
37 Grand Rapids, U.S.A. 42 57N 85 40W
34 Grande Prairie, Can. 55 15N 118 50W
10 Graz, Austria 47 4N 15 27E
39 Great Abaco, I. Bahamas 26 30N 77 20W
26 Great Australian Bight, Australia 33 0S 130 0E
27 Great Barrier Reef, Australia 19 0S 149 0E
34 Great Bear L., Canada 65 0N 120 0W
27 Great Divide, Mts., Australia 23 0S 146 0E
36 Great Falls, U.S.A. 47 29N 111 19W
36 Great Salt L. U.S.A. 41 0N 112 30W
26 Great Sandy Desert, Australia 21 0S 124 0E
34 Great Slave L., Can. 61 30N 114 20W
26 Great Victoria Desert, Australia 29 30S 126 30E
6 Great Yarmouth, Eng. 52 40N 1 45E
39 Greater Antilles, W. Indies 17 40N 74 0W
15 Greece, St. Europe 40 0N 23 0E
37 Green Bay, U.S.A. 44 30N 88 0W
35 Greenland, N. America 66 0N 45 0W
8 Greenock, Scotland 55 57N 4 46W
37 Greensboro, U.S.A. 36 5N 79 47W
39 Grenada I., W. Indies 12 10N 61 40W
12 Grenoble, France 45 12N 5 42E
28 Greymouth, N.Z. 42 29S 171 13E
27 Griffith, Australia 34 14S 145 46E
6 Grimsby, England 53 35N 0 5W
18 Grodno, U.S.S.R. 53 42N 23 52E
10 Groningen, Netherlands 53 15N 6 35E
18 Groznyy, U.S.S.R. 43 20N 45 45E
38 Guadalajara, Mexico 20 40N 103 20W
13 Guadalquiver, R., Spain 38 0N 4 0W
39 Guadeloupe, I., Fr. W. Indies 16 20N 61 40W
13 Guadiana, R., Spain 37 55N 7 39W
13 Guadix, Spain 37 18N 3 11W
39 Guanabacoa, Cuba 23 8N 82 18W
39 Guantánamo, Cuba 20 10N 75 20W
42 Guarapuava, Brazil 25 20S 51 30W
38 Guatemala, st. Central America 15 40N 90 30W
38 Guatemala, Guatemala, 14 40N 90 30
40 Guaviare, R., Colombia 3 30N 71 0W
40 Guayaquil, Ecuador 2 15N 79 52W
38 Guaymas, Mexico 27 50N 111 0W
7 Guernsey, I., Brit. Isles 49 30N 2 35W
7 Guildford, England 51 14N 0 34W
30 Guinea, st., W. Africa 10 20N 10 0W
29 Guinea, G. of, W. Africa 3 0N 2 30E
30 Guinea-Bissau, st., W. Africa 12 0N 15 0W
22 Gujranwala, Pakistan 32 10N 74 12E
18 Guryev, U.S.S.R. 47 5N 52 0E
40 Guyana, St., S. America 5 0N 59 0W
22 Gwalior, India 26 12N 78 10E
33 Gwelo, Rhodesia 19 28S 29 45E
7 Gwent, Co., Wales 51 40N 3 0W
6 Gwynedd, Co., Wales 53 0N 4 0N
27 Gympie, Australia 26 11S 152 38E

H

10 Haarlem, Netherlands 52 23N 4 39E
24 Hachiōji, Japan 35 30N 139 30E
21 Haifa, Israel 32 48N 35 0E
39 Haiti, st., W. Indies 19 6N 72 30W
24 Hakodate, Japan 41 45N 140 44E
21 Halab (Aleppo) Syria 36 12N 37 13E
35 Halifax, Canada 44 38N 63 35W
6 Halifax, England 53 43N 1 51W
10 Halle, E. Germany 51 29N 12 0E
23 Halmahera, I., Indonesia 0 40N 128 0E
17 Halmstad, Sweden 56 37N 12 56E
21 Hamā, Syria 35 5N 36 40E
21 Hamadan, Iran 34 52N 48 32E
17 Hamar, Norway 60 48N 11 7E
24 Hamamatsu, Japan 34 45N 137 45E
10 Hamburg W. Germany 53 32N 9 59E
17 Hämeenlinna, Finland 61 3N 24 26E
35 Hamilton, Canada 43 20N 79 50W
28 Hamilton, N.Z. 37 47S 175 19E
8 Hamilton, Scotland 55 47N 4 2W
16 Hammerfest, Norway 70 33N 23 50E

* *Renamed Kiribati*

7 Hampshire, Co., England 51 3N 1 20W
25 Hangchow, China 30 20N 120 5E
17 Hangö, Finland 59 59N 22 57E
10 Hannover, W. Germany 52 23N 9 43E
23 Hanoi, Vietnam 21 5N 105 40E
16 Haparanda, Sweden 65 52N 24 8E
25 Harbin, China 45 45N 126 41E
16 Härnösand, Sweden 62 38N 18 5E
8 Harris, Scotland 57 50N 6 55W
37 Harrisburg, U.S.A. 40 18N 76 52W
6 Harrogate, England 53 59N 1 32W
37 Hartford, U.S.A. 41 47N 72 41W
6 Hartlepool, England 54 42N 1 11W
7 Harwich, England 51 56N 1 18E
7 Hastings, England 50 51N 0 36E
28 Hastings, N.Z. 39 39S 176 52E
36 Hawaiian Is., Pacific Oc. 20 0N 155 0W
8 Hawick, Scotland 55 25N 2 48W
27 Hawker, Australia 31 59S 138 22E
35 Hearst, Canada 49 40N 83 41W
10 Heidelberg, W. Ger. 49 23N 8 41E
17 Helsingborg, Sweden 56 3N 12 42E
17 Helsingør, Denmark 56 2N 12 35E
17 Helsinki, Finland 60 15N 25 3E
25 Hengyang, China 26 58N 112 25E
21 Herat, Afghanistan 34 20N 62 7E
7 Hereford, England 52 4N 2 42W
7 Hereford & Worcester, Co., England 52 4N 2 43W
38 Hermosillo, Mexico 29 10N 111 0W
7 Hertfordshire, Co., England 51 51N 0 5W
24 Hida-Sammyaku, Japan 36 30N 137 40E
38 Hidalgo del Parral, Mexico 26 10N 104 50W
7 High Wycombe, Eng. 51 37N 0 45W
8 Highland, Co., Scotland 57 30N 5 0W
36 Hilo, Hawaiian Is. 19 42N 155 4W
22 Himalaya, Mts., Asia 29 0N 84 0E
24 Himeji, Japan 34 50N 134 40E
21 Hindu Kush, Ra., Afghan. 36 0N 71 0E
24 Hiroshima, Japan 37 40N 132 30E
39 Hispaniola, I., W. Indies 19 0N 71 0W
17 Hjørring, Denmark 57 29N 9 59E
27 Hobart, Tasmania 42 50S 147 21E
24 Hokkaido, I., Japan 43 30N 143 0E
39 Holguín, Cuba 20 50N 76 20W
6 Holyhead, Wales 53 18N 4 38W
39 Honduras, Rep. Central America 14 40N 86 30W
17 Hønefoss, Norway 60 10N 10 12E
25 Hong Kong, Br. Crown Colony, Asia 22 11N 14 14E
36 Honolulu, Hawaiian Is. 21 25N 157 55W
24 Honshu, I., Japan 36 0N 138 0E
42 Horn, C., Chile 55 50S 67 30W
17 Horsens, Denmark 55 52N 9 50E
17 Horten, Norway 59 25N 10 32E
13 Hospitalet, Spain 41 21N 2 6E
37 Houston, U.S.A. 29 50N 95 20W
7 Hove, England 50 50N 0 10W
22 Howrah, India 22 37N 88 27E
25 Hsiamen, China 24'30N 118 7E
33 Murambo, Angola 12 42S 15 54W
6 Huddersfield, England 53 38N 1 49W
35 Hudson, B., Canada 60 0N 86 0W
37 Hudson, R., U.S.A. 41 35N 74 0W
35 Hudson Str., Canada 62 0N 70 0W
23 Hue, Vietnam 16 60N 107 35E
13 Huelva, Spain 37 18N 6 57W
13 Huesca, Spain 42 8N 0 25W
27 Hughenden, Australia 20 52S 144 10E
35 Hull, Canada 45 20N 75 40W
6 Hull, England 53 45N 0 20W
6 Humber, R., England 53 42N 0 20W
6 Humberside, Co., Eng. 53 40N 0 30W
11 Hungary, Rep. Europe 47 20N 19 20E
37 Huntingdon, U.S.A. 38 20N 82 30W
35 Huron, L., N. America 45 0N 83 0W
25 Hwang-Ho, R., China 40 50N 107 30E
22 Hyderabad, India 17 10N 78 20E
22 Hyderabad, Pakistan 25 23N 68 36E

I

11 Iaşi, Rumania 47 10N 27 40E
30 Ibadan, Nigeria 7 22N 3 58E
40 Ibaqué, Colombia 4 27N 73 14W
13 Ibiza, I., Spain 39 0N 1 30E
16 Iceland, Rep., Europe 65 0N 19 0W
24 Ichinomiya, Japan 35 20N 136 50E
30 Ife, Nigeria 7 30N 4 31E
23 Iloilo, Philippines, 10 45N 122 33E
25 Inchon, S. Korea 37 30N 126 30E
22 India, St., Asia 23 0N 80 0E
20 Indian Ocean 5 0S 75 0E
37 Indianapolis, U.S.A. 39 42N 86 10W
23 Indonesia, Rep., Asia 5 0S 115 0E
22 Indore, India 22 42N 75 53E
22 Indus, R., Pakistan 28 40N 70 10E
27 Ingham, Australia 18 43S 146 10E
33 Inhambane, Moz. 23 51S 35 29E
8 Inner Hebrides, Is., Scotland 58 0N 7 0W
10 Innsbruck, Austria 47 16N 11 23E
28 Invercargill, N.Z. 46 24S 168 24E
8 Inverness, Scotland 57 29N 4 12W
15 Ionian Sea, Europe 37 30N 17 30E
27 Ipswich, Australia 27 38S 152 37E
7 Ipswich, England 52 4N 1 9E
40 Iquique, Chile 20 19S 70 5W
40 Iquitos, Peru 3 45S 73 10W
15 Iráklion, Greece 35 20N 25 12E
21 Iran, st., Asia 33 0N 53 0E
21 Iraq, st., Asia 33 0N 44 0E
9 Ireland, Rep., Europe 53 0N 8 0W
23 Irian Jaya, Indonesia 4 0S 137 0E
5 Irish Sea, Europe 54 0N 5 0W
19 Irkutsk, U.S.S.R. 52 10N 104 20E
8 Islay, I., Scotland 55 46N 6 10W
31 Ismâ'illa, Egypt 30 47N 32 18E
21 Israel, st., Asia 32 30N 32 30E
21 Istanbul, Turkey 41 0N 29 0E
41 Itabuna, Brazil 14 48S 39 16W
14 Itlay, Rep., Europe 42 0N 13 0E
18 Ivanovo, U.S.S.R. 57 5N 41 0E
30 Ivory Coast, st., W. Africa 7 30N 5 0W

30 Iwo, Nigeria 7 39N 4 9E
18 Izhevsk, U.S.S.R. 56 50N 53 0E
21 Izmir, Turkey 38 25N 27 8E

J

22 Jabalpur, India 23 9N 79 58E
37 Jackson, U.S.A. 32 20N 90 10W
37 Jacksonville, U.S.A. 30 15N 81 38W
13 Jaén, Spain 37 44N 3 43W
22 Jaipur, India 20 51N 86 28E
38 Jalapa, Mexico 19 30N 96 50W
39 Jamaica, I., W. Indies 18 10N 77 30W
35 James, .B, Canada 53 30N 80 30W
22 Jamshedpur, India 22 44N 86 20E
24 Japan, st., Asia 36 0N 136 0E
24 Japan, Sea of, Asia 40 0N 135 0E
41 Jau, Brazil 22 10S 48 30W
23 Java, I., Indonesia 7 0S 110 0E
13 Jerez, Spain 36 41N 6 7W
7 Jersey, I., British Isles 49 13N 2 7W
37 Jersey City, U.S.A. 40 41N 74 8W
21 Jerusalem, Israel 31 47N 35 10E
21 Jidda, Saudi Arabia 21 29N 39 16E
41 João Pessoa, Brazil 7 10S 35 0W
22 Jodhpur, India 26 23N 73 2E
* 23 Jogjakarta, Indonesia 6 9S 106 49E
33 Johannesburg, S. Africa 26 10S 28 8E
8 John O'Groats, Scot. 58 39N 3 3W
17 Jönköping, Sweden 57 45N 14 10E
21 Jordan, st., Asia 31 0N 36 0E
17 Jotunheimen, Mts., Norway 61 30N 9 0E
41 Juàzeiro do Norte, Brazil 7 10S 39 18W
41 Juiz de Fora, Brazil 21 43S 43 19W
22 Jullundur, India 31 20N 75 40E
34 Juneau, Alaska 58 21N 134 20W
8 Jura, I., Scotland 56 0N 5 50W
12 Jura, Mts., Europe 46 35N 6 5E
40 Juruá, R., Brazil 5 20S 67 40W
16 Jyväskylä, Finland 62 12N 25 47E

K

21 Kabul, Afghanistan 34 28N 69 18E
30 Kaduna, Nigeria 10 30N 7 21E
24 Kagoshima, Japan 31 36N 130 40E
23 Kaifeng, China 34 45N 114 30E
16 Kajaani, Finland 64 17N 27 46E
33 Kalahari, Desert, Africa 24 0S 22 0E
32 Kalemie, Zaïre 5 55S 29 9E
26 Kalgoorlie, Australia 30 40S 121 22E
18 Kalinin, U.S.S.R. 56 55N 35 55E
18 Kaliningrad, U.S.S.R. 54 42N 20 32E
17 Kalmar, Sweden 56 39N 16 22E
18 Kaluga, U.S.S.R. 54 35N 36 10E
32 Kamina, Zaïre 8 45S 25 0E
34 Kamloops, Canada 50 40N 120 20W
32 Kampala, Uganda 0 20N 32 30E
32 Kananga, Zaïre 5 55S 22 18E
24 Kanazawa, Japan 36 30N 136 38E
21 Kandahar, Afghanistan 31 32N 65 30E
18 Kandalaksha, U.S.S.R. 67 9N 32 30E
22 Kandy, Sri Lanka 7 18N 80 43E
30 Kano, Nigeria 12 0N 8 30E
22 Kanpur, India 26 35N 80 20E
37 Kansas City, U.S.A. 39 0N 94 37W
25 Kaohsiung, Taiwan 22 35N 120 16E
22 Karachi, Pakistan 24 53N 67 0E
18 Karaganda, U.S.S.R. 49 50N 73 0E
22 Karakorum, Mts., India 35 20N 78 0E
21 Karbala, Iraq 32 47N 44 3E
33 Kariba, L. Zambia-Rhodesia 16 40S 28 20E
10 Karl-Marx-Stadt, E. Germany 50 50N 12 55E
17 Karlskrona, Sweden 56 12N 15 42E
10 Karlsruhe, W. Germany 49 3N 8 23E
17 Karlstad, Sweden 59 24N 13 35E
32 Kasai, R., Zaïre 8 20S 22 0E
10 Kassel, W. Germany 51 19N 9 32E
26 Katherine, Australia 14 27S 132 20E
22 Katmandu, Nepal 27 45N 85 12E
27 Katoomba, Australia 33 30N 150 0E
11 Katowice Poland, 50 17N 19 5E
30 Katsina, Nigeria 7 10N 9 20E
17 Kattegat, Str., Denmark 56 50N 11 20E
18 Kaunas, U.S.S.R. 54 54N 23 54E
24 Kawaguchi, Japan 35 52N 138 45E
24 Kawasaki, Japan 35 40N 139 45E
28 Kawerau, N.Z. 38 7S 176 42E
18 Kazan, U.S.S.R. 55 48N 49 3E
15 Kazanlŭk, Bulgaria 42 38N 25 35E
33 Keetmanshoop, S. W. Africa 26 35S 18 8E
16 Keflavik, Iceland 64 2N 22 35W
6 Keighley, England 53 52N 1 54W
18 Kemerovo, U.S.S.R. 55 20N 85 50W
16 Kemi, Finland 65 48N 24 43E
34 Kenora, Canada 49 50N 94 35W
7 Kent, Co., England 51 12N 0 40E
32 Kenya, st., E. Africa 0 5N 37 0E
3 Kerguelen, I., Indian Oc. 48 30S 69 40E
15 Kérkira, I., Greece 39 40N 19 50E
28 Kermadec Is., Pacific Oc. 31 8S 175 16W
21 Kerman, Iarn 30 15N 57 1E
21 Kermanshah, Iran 34 23N 47 0E
9 Kerry, Co., Ireland 52 7N 9 35W
37 Key West, U.S.A. 24 40N 82 0W
19 Kharbarovsk, U.S.S.R. 48 20N 135 0E
18 Kharkov, U.S.S.R. 49 58N 36 20E
31 Khartoum = El Kharṭûm
15 Khaskovo, Bulgaria 41 56N 25 30E
18 Kherson, U.S.S.R. 46 35N 32 35E
15 Khíos, I., Greece 38 23N 29 0E
22 Khulna, Bangladesh 22 45N 89 34E
10 Kiel, W. Germany 54 16N 10 8E
15 Kikládhes, Is., Greece 37 50N 25 0E
9 Kildare, Co., Ireland 53 10N 6 50W
32 Kilimanjaro, Mt., Tanzania 3 4S 37 21E
9 Kilkenny & Co., Ireland 52 40N 7 17W
9 Killarney, Ireland 52 2N 9 30W
8 Kilmarnock, Scotland 55 36N 4 30W
33 Kimberley, S. Africa 28 43N 24 46E
27 King I., Australia 39 40S 144 0E
6 King's Lynn, England 52 45N 0 25E
35 Kingston, Canada 44 20N 76 30W
32 Kinshasha, Zaïre 4 20N 15 15E

19 Kirensk, U.S.S.R. 57 50N 107 55E
25 Kirin, China 43 50N 126 38E
8 Kirkcaldy, Scotland 56 7N 3 10W
35 Kirkland Lake, Canada 48 15N 80 0W
21 Kirkuk, Iraq 35 30N 44 21E
8 Kirkwall, Scotland 58 59N 2 59W
18 Kirov, U.S.S.R. 58 25N 49 40E
18 Kirovogard, U.S.S.R. 48 35N 32 20E
16 Kiruna, Sweden 67 50N 20 20E
32 Kisangani, Zaïre 0 41N 25 11E
18 Kiselevsk, U.S.S.R. 54 5N 86 6E
18 Kishinev, U.S.S.R. 47 1N 28 50E
29 Kismayu, Somalia 0 20S 42 30E
24 Kitakyûshû, Japan 33 50N 130 50E
35 Kitchener, Canada 43 30N 80 30W
33 Kitwe, Zambia 12 50S 28 0E
18 Kiyev, U.S.S.R. 50 30N 30 28E
10 Klagenfurt, Austria 46 38N 14 20E
37 Knoxville, U.S.A. 35 58N 83 57W
24 Kōbe, Japan 34 45N 135 10E
17 København, (Copenhagen) Denmark 55 41N 12 34E
10 Koblenz, W. Germany 50 21N 7 36E
24 Kōchi, Japan 33 30N 133 35E
16 Kokkola, Finlnad 63 50N 23 8E
17 Kolding, Denmark 55 30N 9 29E
22 Kolhapur, India 16 43N 74 15E
10 Köln, W. Germany 50 56N 9 58E
18 Kolomna, U.S.S.R. 55 8N 38 45E
32 Kolwezi, Zaïre 10 40S 25 25E
19 Komsomolsk, U.S.S.R. 50 30N 137 0E
18 Kopeysk, U.S.S.R. 54 55N 61 31E
15 Korab, Mt., Y-slav. 41 44N 20 40E
24 Kōriyama, Japan 37 10N 140 18E
27 Kosciusko, Mt., Australia 36 27S 148 16E
11 Kosice, Czechoslovakia 48 42N 21 15E
18 Kostroma, U.S.S.R. 57 50N 41 58E
25 Kowloon, Hong Kong 22 25N 114 10E
15 Kragujevac, Yugoslavia 44 2N 20 56E
11 Krakow, Poland 50 4N 19 57E
18 Krasnodar, U.S.S.R. 45 5N 38 50E
18 Krasnovodsk, U.S.S.R. 50 0N 52 52E
18 Krasnoyarsk, U.S.S.R. 56 8N 93 0E
18 Kremenchug, U.S.S.R. 49 5N 33 25E
17 Kristiansand, Norway 58 9N 8 1E
16 Kristiansund, Norway 63 10N 7 45E
16 Kristinestad, Finland 62 16N 21 21E
15 Kriti, I., (Crete) Greece 35 15N 25 0E
18 Krivoy Rog, U.S.S.R. 47 51N 33 20E
33 Krugersdorp, S. Africa 26 5S 27 46E
23 Krung Thep (Bangkok) Thailand 13 45N 100 31E
23 Kuala Lumpur, Malaysia 3 9N 101 41E
24 Kumamoto, Japan 32 45N 130 45E
30 Kumasi, Ghana 6 41N 1 38W
32 Kumba, Cameroon 4 36N 9 24E
25 Kunlun Shan, Asia 36 0N 86 30E
25 Kunming, China 25 0N 102 45E
26 Kununurra, Australia 15 40S 128 39E
16 Kuopio, Finland 62 53N 27 35E
24 Kurashiki, Japan 34 40N 133 50E
24 Kure, Japan 33 15N 133 15E
18 Kurgan, U.S.S.R. 55 30N 65 0E
18 Kursk, U.S.S.R. 51 42N 36 11E
18 Kustanai, U.S.S.R. 53 20N 63 45E
21 Kuwait = Al Kuwayt
21 Kuwait, st., Asia 29 30N 47 30E
18 Kuybyshev, U.S.S.R. 53 20N 57 0E
25 Kwangchow, China 23 10N 113 10E
25 Kweiyang, China 26 30N 106 35E
8 Kyle of Lochalsh, Scotland 57 17N 5 43 W
24 Kyushu, I., Japan 32 30N 131 0E

L

39 La Ceiba, Honduras 15 40N 86 50W
13 La Coruña, Spain 43 20N 8 25W
39 La Habana, Cuba 23 8N 82 22W
13 La Linea de la Concepción, Spain 36 15N 5 23W
40 La Paz, Bolivia 16 20S 68 10W
38 La Paz, Mexico 24 10N 110 20W
38 La Piedad, Mexico 20 20N 102 1W
42 La Plata, Argentina 35 0S 57 55W
12 La Rochelle, France 46 10N 1 9W
39 La Romana, Dominican Rep. 18 27N 68 57W
42 La Serena, Chile 29 55S 71 10W
14 La Spézia, Italy 44 8N 9 48E
35 Labrador, Reg., Canada 53 20N 61 0W
23 Labuan, I. Malaysia 5 15N 115 38W
22 Laccadive Is., Indian Oc. 10 0N 72 30E
9 Lagan, R., N. Ireland 54 35N 5 55W
30 Lagos, Nigeria 6 25N 3 27E
13 Lagos, Portugal 37 5N 8 41W
22 Lahore, Pakistan 31 32N 74 22E
17 Lahti, Finland 60 59N 25 45E
37 Lakewood, U.S.A. 41 28N 81 50W
6 Lancashire, Co., England 53 5N 2 30W
6 Lancaster, England 54 3N 2 48W
25 Lanchow, China 36 0N 103 50E
7 Land's End, England 50 4N 5 43W
12 Langrse, France 47 52N 5 20E
37 Lansing, U.S.A. 42 47N 84 32W
9 Laois, Co., Ireland 53 0N 7 20W
23 Laos, st., Asia 17 45N 105 0E
19 Lapter Sea, 'S.S.R. 76 0N 125 0E
14 L'Aquila, Italy 42 21N 13 24E
36 Laredo, U.S.A. 27 34N 99 29W
15 Lárisa, Greece 39 38N 22 28E
17 Larvik, Norway 59 4N 10 0E
30 Las Palmas, Canary Is. 28 10N 15 28W
36 Las Vegas, U.S.A. 36 10N 115 5W
27 Launceston, Australia 41 24S 147 8E
12 Lausanne, Switzerland 46 32N 6 38E
12 Le Havre, France 49 30N 0 5E
12 Le Mans, France 48 0N 0 12E
7 Leamington, England 52 18N 1 32W
21 Lebanon, st., Asia 34 0N 36 0E
15 Lecce, Italy 40 20N 18 10E
6 Leeds, England 53 48N 1 34W
39 Leeward Is., W. Indies 16 30N 63 30W
14 Leghorn = Livorno
7 Leicester & Co., England 52 39N 1 9W
10 Leipzig, E. Germany 51 20N 12 23E
8 Leith, Scotland 55 55N 3 11W
9 Leitrim, Co., Ireland 54 8N 8 0W

10 Léman, L. Switzerland 46 26N 6 30E
18 Leningrad, U.S.S.R. 59 55N 30 20E
18 Leninsk Kuznetskiy U.S.S.R. 55 10N 86 10E
38 León, Mexico 21 7N 101 30W
39 León, Nicaragua 12 20N 86 51W
13 León, Spain 42 38N 5 34W
13 Lérida, Spain 41 37N 0 39E
8 Lerwick, Scotland 60 10N 1 10W
33 Lesotho, st., Africa 29 40S 28 0E
15 Lésvos, I., Greece 26 0N 39 15E
34 Lethbridge, Canada 49 45N 112 45W
28 Levin, N.Z. 40 37S 175 18E
21 Levkösia, Cyprus 35 10N 33 25E
8 Lewis, I., Scotland 58 10N 6 40W
37 Lexington, U.S.A. 38 6N 84 30W
25 Lhasa, Tibet, China 29 40N 91 10E
30 Liberia, st., W. Africa 6 30N 9 30W
32 Libreville, Gabon 0 25N 9 26E
31 Libya, st., N. Africa 28 30N 17 30E
10 Liechtenstein, st., Europe 47 8N 9 35E
9 Liffey, R., Ireland 53 21N 6 20W
9 Lifford, Ireland 54 50N 7 30W
14 Ligurian Sea, Europe 43 20N 9 0E
32 Likasi, Zaïre 10 55S 26 48E
12 Lille, France 50 38N 3 3E
17 Lillehammer, Norway 61 8N 10 30E
33 Lilongwe, Malawi 14 0S 33 48E
40 Lima, Peru 12 0S 77 0W
37 Lima, U.S.A. 40 42N 84 5W
9 Limerick & Co., Ireland 52 40N 8 38W
15 Límnos, I., Greece 39 50N 25 15E
12 Limoges, France 45 50N 1 15E
39 Limón, Costa Rica 10 0N 83 2W
33 Limpopo, R. Africa 24 15S 32 45E
13 Linares, Spain 38 10N 3 40W
6 Lincoln & Co., England 53 11N 0 20W
37 Lincoln, U.S.A. 40 50N 96 42W
17 Linköping, Sweden 58 28N 15 36E
8 Linnhe, L., Scotland 56 36N 5 25W
10 Linz, Austria 48 18N 14 18E
14 Lípari, Is., Italy 38 40N 15 0E
18 Lipetsk, U.S.S.R. 52 45N 39 35E
13 Lisboa, Portugal 38 42N 9 10W
9 Lisburn, N. Ireland 54 30N 6 2W
27 Lismore, Australia 28 44S 153 21E
9 Listowel, Ierland 52 27N 9 30W
37 Little Rock, U.S.A. 34 41N 92 10W
6 Liverpool, England 53 25N 3 0W
33 Livingstone, Zambia 17 50N 25 50E
14 Livorno, Italy 43 32N 10 18E
7 Lizard, Pt., England 49 57N 5 11W
14 Ljubljana, Yugoslavia 46 4N 14 33E
33 Lobito, Angola 12 18S 13 35E
40 Llanos, S. America 3 25N 71 35W
11 Lódz, Poland 51 45N 19 27E
16 Lofoten, Is., Norway 68 20N 14 0E
13 Logroño, Spain 42 28N 2 32W
12 Loire, R., France 47 25N 0 20W
23 Lombok, I., Indonesia 8 35S 116 20E
30 Lomé, Togo 6 9N 1 20E
35 London, Canada 43 0N 81 15W
7 London, England 51 30N 0 5W
9 Londonderry, N. Ireland 55 0N 7 20W
42 Londrina, Brazil 23 0S 51 10W
36 Long Beach, U.S.A. 33 46N 118 12W
37 Long I., U.S.A. 40 50N 73 20W
9 Longford, & Co., Ire. 53 43N 7 50W
13 Lorca, Spain 37 41N 1 42W
12 Lorient, France 47 45N 3 23W
36 Los Angeles, U.S.A. 34 0N 118 10W
8 Lothian, Co., Scotland 55 55N 3 15W
37 Louisville, U.S.A. 38 15N 85 45W
33 Lourenço Marques = Maputo, Mozambique 25 57S 32 34E
9 Louth, Co., Ireland 53 55N 6 30W
28 Lower Hutt, N.Z. 41 10S 174 55E
7 Lowestoft, England 52 29N 1 44E
25 Loyang, China 34 40N 112 28E
32 Lualaba, R., Zaïre 5 45S 26 50E
32 Luanda, Angola 8 58S 13 9E
33 Luanshya, Zambia 13 20S 28 8E
36 Lubbock, U.S.A. 33 40N 102 0W
11 Lublin, Poland 51 12N 22 38E
33 Lubumbashi, Zaïre 11 32S 27 28E
14 Lucca, Italy 43 50N 10 30E
25 Luchow, China 28 54N 105 17E
22 Lucknow, India 26 50N 81 0E
33 Lüderitz, S.W. Africa 26 37S 15 9E
22 Ludhiana, India 30 57N 75 56E
13 Lugo, Spain 43 2N 7 35W
16 Luleå, Sweden 65 35N 22 10E
33 Lusaka, Zambia 15 25S 28 15E
25 Lu-Ta, China 39 0N 121 31E
7 Luton, England 51 53N 0 24W
10 Luxembourg, st. Europe 50 0N 6 0E
10 Luzern, Switzerland 47 3N 8 18E
23 Luzon, I. Philippines 16 30N 121 30E
18 Lvov, U.S.S.R. 49 40N 24 0E
* 22 Lyallpur, Pakistan 31 30N 73 5E
16 Lycksele, Sweden 64 38N 18 40E
37 Lynchburg, U..SA. 37 23N 79 10W
12 Lyon, France 45 46N 4 50E
28 Lyttleton, N.Z. 43 35S 172 44E

M

25 Macau, China 22 16N 113 35E
41 Maceió, Brazil 9 40S 35 41W
9 Macgillycuddy's Reeks, Mts., Ireland 52 2N 9 45W
27 Mackay, Australia 21 36S 148 39E
34 Mackenzie, R., Can. 69 10N 134 20W
37 Macon, U.S.A. 32 50N 83 37W
9 Macroom, Ireland 51 54N 8 57W
33 Madagascar, st., Africa 19 0S 46 0E
30 Madeira, Is. Atlantic Oc. 32 50N 17 0W
40 Madeira, R., Brazil 5 30S 61 20W
37 Madison, U.S.A. 43 5N 89 25W
22 Madras, India 13 8N 80 19E
13 Madrid, Spain 40 25N 3 45W
22 Madurai, India 9 55N 78 10E
24 Maebashi, Japan 36 30N 139 0E
40 Magdalena, R., Colombia 8 30N 74 0W
10 Magdeburg, E. Germany 52 8N 11 36E
18 Magnitogorsk, U.S.S.R. 53 20N 59 0E

7 Maidstone, England 51 16N 0 31E
31 Maiduguri, Nigeria 12 0N 13 20E
10 Mainz, W. Germany 50 0N 8 17E
27 Maitland, Australia 32 44S 151 36E
23 Makasar, Str. of, Indon. 1 0S 118 20E
18 Makeyevka, U.S.S.R. 48 0N 38 0E
21 Makkah (Mecca), Saudi Arabia 21 30N 39 54E
23 Malacca, Str. of, Indonesia 3 0N 101 0E
13 Malaga, Spain 36 43N 4 23W
33 Malagasy Rep. st. = Madagascar 19 0S 46 0E
33 Malawi, L., Malawi 12 0S 34 30E
33 Malawi, st., Africa 13 0S 34 0E
23 Malaysia, Fed. of, Asia 5 23N 110 0E
22 Maldive Is., Indian Oc. 6 50N 73 0E
30 Mali, st., W. Africa 17 0N 4 0W
9 Malin Hd., Ireland 55 18N 7 16W
8 Mallaig, Scotland 57 0N 5 50W
13 Mallorca, I., Spain 39 30N 3 0E
9 Mallow, Ireland 52 8N 8 40W
17 Malmö, Sweden 55 33N 13 8E
14 Malta, st. Mediterranean Sea 35 50N 14 30E
6 Man, I. of, U.K. 54 15N 4 30W
23 Manado, Indonesia 1 40N 125 45E
39 Managua, Nicaragua 12 0N 86 20W
40 Manaus, Brazil 3 0S 60 0W
6 Manchester, England 53 30N 2 15W
37 Manchester, U.S.A. 42 58N 71 29W
22 Mandale, Burma 22 0N 96 10E
23 Manila, Philippines 14 40N 121 3E
34 Manitoba, L., Canada 50 40N 98 30W
40 Manizales, Colombia 5 10N 75 30W
10 Mannheim, W. Ger. 49 28N 8 29E
6 Mansfield, England 53 8N 1 12W
14 Mantova, (Mantua) Italy 45 10N 10 47E
28 Manukau, N.Z. 37 0S 174 50E
39 Manzanillo, Cuba 20 20N 77 10W
33 Maputo, Mozambique 25 57S 32 34E
42 Mar del Plata, Argentina 38 0S 57 30W
40 Maracaibo, Venezuela 10 37N 71 45W
40 Maracaibo, L. de, Ven. 9 40N 71 30W
40 Maracay, Venezuela 10 20N 67 35W
40 Margarita, I. de, Ven. 11 0N 64 0W
7 Margate, England 51 23N 1 24E
28 Maria van Diemen, C., N.Z. 34 29S 172 40E
3 Mariana Is., Pacific Oc. 17 0N 145 0E
39 Marianao, Cuba 23 8N 82 24W
14 Maribor, Yugoslavia 46 36N 15 40E
41 Marilia, Brazil 22 0S 50 0W
42 Maringá, Brazil 23 35S 51 50W
2 Marquesas Is., Pacific Oc. 9 30S 140 0W
30 Marrakech, Morocco 31 40N 8 0W
12 Marseille, France 43 18N 5 23E
3 Marshall Is., Pacific Oc. 9 0N 171 0E
39 Martinique, I., Fr. W. Indies 14 40N 61 0W
27 Maryborough, Austral. 25 31S 152 37E
39 Masaya, Nicaragua 12 0N 86 7W
21 Masqat, Oman 23 37N 58 36E
12 Massif Central, Mts., Fr. 45 30N 2 21E
28 Masterton, N.Z. 40 56S 175 39E
32 Matadi, Zaïre 5 52S 13 31E
39 Matagalpa, Nicaragua 13 10N 85 40W
38 Matamoros, Mexico 25 50N 97 30W
39 Matanzas, Cuba 23 0N 81 40W
24 Matsue, Japan 35 25N 133 10E
24 Matsuyama, Japan 33 45N 132 45E
30 Mauritania, st., Africa 20 0N 10 0W
29 Mauritius, st., Indian Oc. 20 0S 57 0E
39 Mayagüez, Puerto Rico 18 11N 67 8W
18 Maykop, U.S.S.R. 44 35N 40 25E
9 Mayo, Co., Ireland 53 47N 9 7W
38 Mazatlán, Mexico 23 10N 106 30W
32 Mbandaka, Zaïre 0 1S 18 18E
9 Meath, Co., Ireland 53 32N 6 40W
21 Mecca = Makkah
23 Medan, Indonesia 3 40N 98 38E
40 Medellín, Colombia 6 20N 75 45W
34 Medicine Hat, Canada 50 0N 110 45W
21 Medina = Al Madinah
4 Mediterranean Sea, Europe 35 0N 15 0E
22 Meerut, India 29 1N 77 50E
30 Meknés, Morocco 33 57N 5 39W
23 Mekong, R., Asia 18 0N 104 15E
27 Melbourne, Australia 37 40S 145 0E
30 Melilla Sp. Morocco 35 21N 2 57W
18 Melitopol, U.S.S.R. 46 50N 35 22E
26 Melville I., Australia 11 30S 131 0E
37 Memphis, U.S.A. 35 7N 90 0W
6 Menai, Str., Wales 53 7N 4 20W
42 Mendoza, Argentina 32 50S 68 52W
13 Menorca, I., Spain 40 0N 4 0E
42 Mercedes, Uruguay 33 12S 58 0W
23 Mergui Arch, Burma 11 30N 97 30E
38 Mérida, Mexico 20 50N 89 40W
6 Merseyside, Co., England 53 30N 3 0W
7 Merthyr Tydfil, Wales 51 45N 3 23W
14 Messina, & Str., Italy 38 10N 15 32E
33 Messina, S. Africa 22 20S 30 12E
12 Metz, France 49 8N 6 10E
38 Mexicali, Mexico 32 40N 115 30W
38 Mexico, st., America 20 0N 100 0N
38 Mexico, G. of, Central America 25 0N 90 0W
38 Mexico City, Mexico 19 20N 99 10W
37 Miami, U.S.A. 25 52N 80 15W
18 Miass, U.S.S.R. 54 59N 60 6E
37 Michigan, L., N. America 44 0N 87 0W
7 Mid Glamorgan, Co., Wales 51 35N 3 30W
33 Middelburg, S. Africa 31 30S 25 0E
6 Middlesbrough, England 54 34N 1 13W
36 Midland, U.S.A. 32 0N 102 3W
2 Midway I., Pacific Oc. 28 0N 178 0W
13 Mieres, Spain 43 18N 5 48W
14 Milano, (Milan) Italy 45 28N 9 10E
27 Mildura, Australia 34 8S 142 7E
7 Milford Haven, Wales 51 43N 5 2W
37 Milwaukee, U.S.A. 43 9N 87 58W
38 Minatitlán, Mexico 17 58N 94 35W
23 Mindanao, I., Philippines 8 0N 125 0E
37 Minneapolis, U.S.A. 44 58N 93 20W
18 Minsk, U.S.S.R. 53 52N 27 30E

11 Miskolc, Hungary 48 7N 20 50E
37 Mississippi, R., U.S.A. 41 0N 91 0W
36 Missouri, R., U.S.A. 38 40N 91 45W
9 Mizen Hd., Ireland 51 27N 9 50W
37 Mobile, U.S.A. 30 41N 88 3W
32 Mobutu Sese Seko, L., Africa 1 30N 31 0E
33 Moçambique, Mozam. 15 3S 40 42E
33 Moçambique, st. Africa 14 45S 38 30E
33 Moçâmedes, Angola 16 35S 12 30E
14 Módena, Italy 44 39N 10 55E
27 Moe, Australia 38 12S 146 19E
29 Mogadishu, Somalia 2 2N 45 25E
18 Mogilev, U.S.S.R. 53 55N 30 18E
17 Mölndal, Sweden 57 40N 12 3E
32 Mombasa, Kenya 4 0S 39 35E
12 Monaco, principality, Europe 43 36N 7 23E
9 Monaghan & Co., 54 15N 6 58W
38 Monclova, Mexico 26 50N 101 30W
35 Moncton, Canada 46 7N 64 51W
25 Mongolia, Rep., Asia 47 0N 103 0E
30 Monrovia, Liberia 6 18N 10 47W
12 Monte Carlo, Monaco 43 46N 7 23E
39 Montego Bay, Jamaica 18 30N 78 0W
38 Monterrey, Mexico 25 40N 100 30W
41 Montes Claros, Brazil 16 30S 43 50W
42 Montevideo, Uruguay 34 50S 56 11W
37 Montgomery, U.S.A. 32 20N 86 20W
12 Montluçon, France 46 22N 2 36E
12 Montpellier, France 43 37N 3 52E
35 Montreal, Canada 45 31N 73 34W
12 Montreuil, France 50 27N 1 45W
8 Montrose, Scotland 56 43N 2 28W
34 Moose Jaw, Canada 50 30N 105 30W
15 Morava, R., Cz. 49 50N 16 50E
8 Moray Firth, Scotland 57 50N 3 30W
6 Morecambe, England 54 5N 2 52W
38 Morelia, Mexico 19 40N 101 11W
30 Morocco, st., N. Africa 32 0N 5 0W
18 Moscow = Moskva
10 Mosel, R., Germany 49 48N 6 45E
16 Mosjøen, Norway 65 52N 13 20E
18 Moskva, U.S.S.R. 55 45N 37 35E
17 Moss, Norway 59 27N 10 40E
33 Mosselbaai, S. Africa 34 11S 22 8E
21 Mosul = Al Mawsil
17 Motala. Sweden 58 32N 15 1E
8 Motherwell, Scotland 55 48N 4 0W
27 Mount Gambier, Australia 37 38S 140 44E
27 Mount Isa, Australia 20 42S 139 26E
26 Mount Magnet, Australia 28 2S 117 47E
9 Mourne, Mts., N. Ire. 54 10N 6 0W
33 Mozambique Chan., Africa 20 0S 39 0E
33 Mozambique, Rep. Africa 23 30S 32 30E
32 Mtwara, Tanzania 10 20S 40 20E
33 Mufulira, Zambia 12 30S 28 0E
12 Mulhouse, France 47 44N 7 20E
8 Mull, I., Scotland 56 27N 6 0W
9 Mullinger, Ireland 53 31N 7 20W
22 Multan, Pakistan 30 15N 71 30E
10 Munchen, W. Germany 48 8N 11 33E
10 Münster, W. Germany 51 58N 7 37E
13 Murcia, Spain 38 2N 1 10W
18 Murmansk, U.S.S.R. 68 57N 33 10E
24 Muroran, Japan 42 25N 141 0E
27 Murray, R., Australia 35 50S 147 40E
21 Muscat = Masqat
32 Mweru, L., Zambia 9 0S 29 0E
22 Mysore, India 13 15N 77 0E

N

9 Naas, Ireland 53 12N 6 40W
24 Nagano, Japan 36 40N 138 10E
24 Nagasaki, Japan 32 47N 129 50E
24 Nagoya, Japan 35 10N 136 50E
22 Nagpur, India 21 8N 79 10E
32 Nairobi, Kenya 1 20S 36 50E
32 Nakuru, Kenya 0 15S 36 5E
16 Namsos, Norway 64 28N 11 35E
25 Nan Shan, China 38 0N 98 0E
34 Nanaimo, Canada 49 10N 124 0W
12 Nancy, France 48 42N 6 12E
25 Nanking, China 32 10N 118 50E
12 Nantes, France 47 12N 1 33W
28 Napier, N.Z. 39 30S 176 56E
14 Napoli (Naples) Italy 40 40N 14 5E
12 Narbonne, France 43 11N 3 0E
22 Narmada, R., India 22 40N 77 30E
27 Narrandera, Australia 34 42S 146 31E
26 Narrogin, Australia 32 58S 117 14E
16 Narvik, Norway 68 27N 17 35E
37 Nashville, U.S.A. 36 12N 86 46W
22 Nasik, India 20 2N 73 50E
39 Nassau, Bahamas 25 0N 77 30W
31 Nasser, L., Egypt 23 0N 32 30E
17 Nässjö, Sweden 57 38N 14 45E
41 Natal, Brazil 5 47S 35 13W
38 Navojoa, Mexico 27 0N 109 30W
15 Naxos, I., Greece 37 5N 25 30E
31 Ndjamena, Chad 12 4N 15 8E
33 Ndola, Zambia 13 0S 28 34E
9 Neagh, L., N. Ireland 54 35N 6 25W
42 Negro, R., Brazil 0 25S 64 0W
28 Nelson, N.Z. 41 18S 173 16E
9 Nenagh, Ireland 52 52N 8 11W
22 Nepal, St., Asia 28 0N 84 30E
8 Ness, L., Scotland 57 15N 4 30W
10 Netherlands, King. Europe 52 0N 5 30E
12 Nevers, France 47 0N 3 9E
37 New Bedford, U.S.A. 41 40N 70 52W
28 New Brighton, N.Z. 43 29S 172 43E
3 New Britain, I., Pacific Oc. 6 0S 151 0E
3 New Caledonia, I., Pacific Oc. 21 0S 165 0E
27 New England Ra., Australia 29 30S 152 0E
3 New Guinea, I., Australasia 4 0S 136 0E
37 New Haven, U.S.A. 41 20N 72 54W
* 3 New Hebrides Is., Pacific Oc. 15 0S 168 0E
3 New Ireland, I., Pacific Oc. 3 0S 151 30E
27 New Norfolk, Australia 44 46S 147 2E
37 New Orleans, U.S.A. 30 0N 90 0W

* *Renamed Yogyakarta*

* *Renamed Shah Faisalabad*

* *Renamed Vanuatu*

28 New Plymouth, N.Z. 39 4S 174 5E	
39 New Providence, I., Bahamas 25 0N 77 30W	
37 New York, U.S.A. 40 45N 74 0W	
28 New Zealand, st., 40 0S 175 0E	
37 Newark, U.S.A. 40 41N 74 12W	
27 Newcastle, Australia 32 52S 151 49E	
6 Newcastle, England 54 58N 1 37W	
6 Newcastle-under-Lyme, England 53 2N 2 15W	
35 Newfoundland, I., Can. 48 28N 56 0W	
7 Newhaven, England, 50 47N 0 4E	
7 Newmarket, England 52 15N 0 23E	
7 Newport, Wales 52 1N 4 51W	
37 Newport Mews, U.S.A. 37 0N 76 25W	
7 Newtownards, N. Ire. 54 37N 5 40W	
37 Niagara Falls, N. Amer. 43 5N 79 5W	
30 Niamey, Niger 13 27N 2 6E	
39 Nicaragua, st. Central America 11 40N 85 30W	
12 Nice, France 43 42N 7 14E	
22 Nicobar, Is., India 9 0N 93 0E	
31 Nicosia = Levkôsia	
30 Niger, st., Africa 15 30N 10 0E	
30 Niger, R., Africa 13 35N 7 0E	
30 Nigeria, st., W. Africa 8 30N 8 0E	
24 Niigata, Japan 37 58N 139 0E	
10 Nijmegen, Netherlands 51 50N 5 52E	
18 Nikolayev, U.S.S.R. 46 58N 32 7E	
31 Nile, R., Egypt 27 30N 30 30E	
12 Nîmes, France 43 50N 4 23E	
25 Ningpo, China 29 50N 121 30E	
35 Nipigon, L., Canada 49 40N 88 30W	
15 Niš, Yugoslavia 43 19N 21 58E	
24 Nishinomiya, Japan 34 45N 135 20E	
41 Niteroi, Brazil 22 52S 43 0W	
18 Nizhniy Tagil, U.S.S.R. 57 45N 60 0E	
38 Nogales, Meixco 31 36N 94 29W	
6 Nome, Alaska 64 35N 165 0E	
6 Norfolk, Co., England 52 39N 1 0E	
37 Norfolk, U.S.A. 42 3N 97 25W	
3 Norfolk I., Pacific Oc. 28 58S 168 3E	
27 Normanton, Australia 17 40S 141 10E	
17 Norrköping, Sweden 58 35N 16 10E	
34 North Battlefield, Canada 52 50N 108 10W	
35 North Bay, Canada 46 20N 79 30W	
5 North Chan., British Isles 55 0N 5 30W	
28 North I., N.Z. 38 0S 175 0E	
25 North Korea, St., Asia 40 0N 127 0E	
4 North Sea, Europe 55 0N 4 9E	
8 North Uist, I., Scotland 57 40N 7 15W	
6 North York Moors, England 54 25N 0 50W	
7 North Yorkshire, Co., England 54 20N 1 30W	
26 Northam, Australia 31 55S 116 42W	
7 Northampton & Co., 52 14N 0 54W	
6 Northern Ireland, United Kingdom 54 45N 7 0W	
6 Northumberland, Co., England 55 12N 2 0W	
16 Norway, King. Europe 67 0N 11 0E	
6 Norwich, England 52 38N 1 17E	
6 Nottingham & Co., 52 57N 1 10W	
3 Nouméa, New Caledonia 22 17S 166 30E	
33 Nova Lisboa, see Huambo, Angola 12 42S 15 54W	
14 Novara, Italy 45 27N 8 36E	
18 Novaya Zemlya, Is. U.S.S.R. 75 0N 56 0E	
18 Novgorod, U.S.S.R. 58 30N 31 25E	
15 Novi Sad, Yugoslavia 45 18N 19 52E	
18 Novokuznetsk, U.S.S.R. 55 0N 83 5E	
18 Novomoskovsk, U.S.S.R. 54 5N 38 15E	
18 Novorossiysk, U.S.S.R. 44 43N 37 52E	
18 Novosibirsk, U.S.S.R. 55 0N 83 5E	
38 Nueva Rosita, Mexico 28 0N 101 20W	
1 Nuneaton, England 52 32 1 29W	
10 Nürnberg, W. Germany 49 26N 11 5E	
33 Nyasa, L., Africa 12 0S 34 30E	

O

36 Oahu, I., Hawaiian Is. 21 30N 158 0W	
37 Oak Ridge, U.S.A. 36 1N 84 5W	
36 Oakland, U.S.A. 37 50N 122 18W	
28 Oamaru, N.Z. 45 5S 170 59E	
38 Oaxaca, Mexico 17 2N 96 40W	
18 Ob, R., U.S.S.R. 62 40N 66 0E	
8 Oban, Scotland 56 25N 5 30W	
40 Occidental, Cordillera, Colombia 5 0N 76 0W	
17 Odense, Denmark 55 26N 10 26E	
18 Odessa, U.S.S.R. 41 30S 30 45E	
15 Odra, R. Poland 52 40N 14 28E	
7 Offaly, Co., Ireland 53 15N 7 30W	
30 Ogbomosho, Nigeria 8 1N 3 29E	
36 Ogden, U.S.A. 41 13N 112 1W	
37 Ohio, R., U.S.A. 39 40N 80 50W	
24 Ōita, Japan 33 15N 131 36E	
33 Okavango Swamps, Botswana 19 30S 23 0E	
24 Okayama, Japan 34 40N 133 44E	
24 Okazaki, Japan 34 36N 137 0E	
21 Okhotsk, Sea of, Asia 55 0N 145 0E	
37 Oklahoma City, U.S.A. 35 25N 97 30W	
17 Öland, I., Sweden 56 45N 16 50E	
10 Oldenburg, W. Germany 53 10N 8 10E	
6 Oldham, England 53 33N 2 8W	
15 Ólimbos, Oros, (Olympus) Greece 40 6N 22 23E	
15 Olympia, Greece 37 39N 21 39E	
21 Oman, G. of, S.W. Asia 24 30N 58 30E	
21 Oman, Sultanate, Asia 23 0N 58 0E	
9 Omagh, N. Ireland 54 36N 7 20W	
37 Omaha, U.S.A. 41 15N 96 0W	
31 Omdurmân, Sudan 15 40N 32 28E	
24 Omiya, Japan 36 0N 139 32E	
18 Omsk, U.S.S.R. 55 0N 73 38E	
28 Onehunga, N.Z. 36 55N 174 50E	
30 Onitsha, Nigeria 6 6N 6 42E	
35 Ontario, L., N. America 43 40N 78 0W	
11 Oradea, Rumania 47 2N 21 58E	
30 Oran, Algeria 36 45N 0 39W	

33 Orange, R., S. Africa 29 50S 24 45E	
33 Orange, R., S. Africa 28 30S 18 0E	
18 Ordzhonikidze, U.S.S.R. 43 0N 44 30E	
17 Orebro, Sweden 59 20N 15 18E	
18 Orel, U.S.S.R. 52 57N 36 3E	
18 Orenburg, U.S.S.R. 52 0N 55 5E	
13 Orense, Spain 42 19N 7 55W	
12 Orléans, France 47 54N 1 52E	
40 Orinoco, R., Venezuela 8 0N 65 30W	
38 Orizaba, Mexico 18 50N 97 10W	
8 Orkney, Is., Scotland 59 0N 3 0W	
37 Orlando, U.S.A. 28 30N 81 25W	
16 Örnsköldsvik, Sweden 63 17N 18 50E	
18 Orsha, U.S.S.R. 54 30N 30 25E	
18 Orsk, U.S.S.R. 51 20N 58 34E	
40 Oruro, Bolivia 18 0S 67 19W	
24 Osaka, Japan 34 40N 135 30E	
30 Oshogbo, Nigeria 7 48N 4 37E	
15 Osijek, Yugoslavia 43 34N 18 41E	
17 Oskarshamn, Sweden 57 15N 16 25E	
17 Cslo, Norway 59 53N 10 52E	
16 Östersund, Sweden 63 10N 14 45E	
11 Ostrava, Czechoslovakia 49 51N 18 18E	
15 Otranto, Str. of, Adriatic Sea 40 15N 18 40E	
35 Ottawa, Canada 45 27N 75 42W	
30 Ouagadougou, Upper Volta 12 25N 1 30W	
32 Oubangi, R., Zaïre 1 0N 17 50E	
30 Oujda, Morocco 34 45N 2 0W	
16 Oulu, Finland 64 25N 27 30E	
7 Ouse, R., England 52 12N 0 7E	
13 Oviedo, Spain 43 25N 5 50W	
8 Outer Hebrides, Is., Scotland	
7 Oxford & Co., 51 45N 1 15W	
30 Oyo, Nigeria 7 46N 3 56E	

P

38 Pachuca, Mexico 20 10N 98 40W	
2 Pacific Ocean 10 0N' 140 0W	
22 Padang, Indonesia 1 0S 100 20E	
14 Pádova, Italy 45 24N 11 52E	
22 Pakistan, St., Asia 30 0N 70 0E	
22 Palawan, I., Philippines 10 0N 119 0E	
22 Palembang, Indonesia 3 0S 104 50E	
13 Palencia, Spain 42 1N 4 34W	
14 Palermo, Italy 38 8N 13 20E	
13 Palma, Spain 39 33N 2 39E	
28 Palmerston North, N.Z. 40 21S 175 39E	
40 Palmira, Colombia 3 32N 76 16W	
13 Pamplona, Spain 42 48N 1 38W	
38 Panama, Panama 9 0N 79 25W	
39 Panama, Rep., Central America 9 0N 79 35W	
22 Panay, I., Philippines 11 0N 122 30E	
14 Pantelleria, I., Italy 36 52N 12 0E	
25 Paotow, China 40 4S 110 0E	
3 Papua New Guinea, st., Australasia 8 0S 145 0E	
42 Paraguay, R., Paraguay 24 30S 58 20W	
42 Paraguay, Rep., S. Amer. 23 0S 57 0W	
41 Paramaribo, Surinam 5 50N 55 10W	
42 Paraná, Argentina 32 0S 60 30W	
42 Paraná, R., Argentine 33 43S 59 15W	
12 Paris, France 48 50N 2 20E	
27 Parkes, Australia 33 9S 148 11E	
14 Parma, Italy 44 50N 10 20E	
35 Parry Sound, Canada 45 20N 80 0W	
36 Pasadena, U.S.A. 34 5N 118 0W	
23 Patna, India 23 35N 85 18E	
15 Patrai, Greece 38 14N 21 47E	
12 Pau, France 43 19N 0 25W	
14 Pavia, Italy 45 10N 9 10E	
18 Pavlodar, U.S.S.R. 52 33N 77 0E	
15 Pazardzhik, Bulgaria 42 12N 24 20E	
11 Pécs, Hungary 46 5N 18 15E	
25 Peiping, China 39 50N 116 20E	
22 Pekalongan, Indonesia 6 53S 109 40E	
41 Pelotas, Brazil 31 42S 52 23W	
35 Pembroke, Wales 51 40N 5 0W	
22 Penang, I., Malaysia 5 25N 100 15E	
25 Pengpu, China 33 0N 117 25E	
18 Penki, China 41 20N 123 50E	
6 Pennines, Rd., England 54 50N 2 20W	
34 Penticton, Canada 49 30N 119 30W	
8 Pentland Firth, 58 43N 3 10W	
18 Penza, U.S.S.R. 53 15N 45 5E	
7 Penzance, England 50 7N 5 32W	
37 Peoria, U.S.A. 40 40N 89 40W	
40 Pereira, Colombia 4 50N 75 40W	
18 Perm, U.S.S.R. 58 0N 56 10E	
12 Perpignan, France 42 42N 2 53E	
21 Persian G., Asia 27 0N 50 0E	
26 Perth, Australia 31 57S 115 52E	
8 Perth, Scotland 56 24N 3 27W	
40 Peru, Rep., S. America 8 0S 75 0W	
14 Perúgia, Italy 43 6N 12 24E	
18 Pervouralsk, U.S.S.R. 56 55N 60 0E	
14 Pésaro, Italy 43 55N 12 53E	
14 Pescara, Italy 42 28N 14 13E	
22 Peshawar, Pakistan 34 2N 71 37E	
35 Peterboro', Canada 44 20N 78 20W	
27 Peterborough, Australia 33 0S 138 45E	
7 Peterborough, England 52 35N 0 14W	
8 Peterhead, Scotland 57 30N 1 49W	
21 Petone, N.Z. 41 13S 174 53E	
18 Petropavlovsk, U.S.S.R. 55 0N 69 0E	
21 Petropavlovsk-Kamchatskiy, U.S.S.R. 53 16N 159 0E	
18 Petrozavodsk, U.S.S.R. 61 41N 34 20E	
23 Phan Bho Chi Minh, Vietnam 10 58N 106 40E	
37 Philadelphia, U.S.A. 40 0N 75 10W	
22 Philippines, Rep., Asia 12 0N 123 0E	
23 Phnom Penh, Cambodia 11 33N 104 55E	
36 Phoenix, U.S.A. 33 30N 112 10W	
2 Phoenix Is., Pacific Oc. 3 30S 172 0W	
14 Piacenza, Italy 45 3N 9 41E	
28 Picton, N.Z. 41 18S 174 3E	
38 Piedras Negras, Mexico 28 35N 100 35W	
33 Pietermaritzburg, S. Africa 23 54S 29 25E	
33 Pietersburg, S. Africa 23 54S 29 25E	

39 Pinar del Rio, Cuba 22 26N 83 40W	
15 Pindos Oros, Greece 40 0N 21 0E	
41 Piracicaba, Brazil 22 45S 47 30W	
15 Piraeus = Piraiévs	
15 Piraiévs, Greece 37 57N 23 42E	
14 Pisa, Italy 43 43N 10 23E	
16 Pistóia, Italy 43 57N 10 53E	
2 Pitcairn I., Pacific Oc. 25 5S 130 5W	
16 Piteå, Sweden 65 55N 21 25E	
37 Pitlochry, Scotland 56 43N 3 43W	
37 Pittsburgh, U.S.A. 40 25N 79 55W	
40 Piura, Peru 5 5S 80 45W	
42 Plata, Rio de la, S. America 35 30S 56 0W	
36 Platte, R., U.S.A. 41 0N 98 0W	
10 Plauen, W. Germany 50 29N 12 9E	
10 Plenty, B. of, N.Z. 37 45S 177 0E	
15 Pleven, Bulgaria 43 26N 24 37E	
11 Ploieşti, Rumania 44 57N 26 5E	
15 Plovdir, Bulgaria 42 8N 24 44E	
7 Plymouth, England 50 23N 4 9W	
10 Plzen, Czechoslovakia 49 5N 13 22E	
14 Po, R., Italy 45 0N 10 45E	
39 Pointe-à-Pitre, Guadaloupe 16 10N 61 30W	
32 Pointe-Noire, Congo 4 48S 12 0E	
12 Poitiers, France 46 35N 0 20W	
11 Poland, st., Europe 52 0N 20 0E	
18 Poltava, U.S.S.R. 49 35N 34 35E	
39 Ponce, Puerto Rico 18 0N 66 50W	
41 Ponta Grossa, Brazil 25 0S 50 10W	
13 Pontevedra, Spain 42 26N 8 40W	
22 Pontianak, Indonesia 0 3S 109 15E	
7 Poole, England 50 42N 2 2W	
23 Poona, India 18 29N 73 57E	
16 Pori, Finland 61 27N 21 50E	
18 Port Augusta, Australia 32 30S 137 50E	
28 Port Chalmers, N.Z. 45 49S 170 30E	
33 Port Elizabeth, S. Africa 33 58S 25 40E	
8 Port Glasgow, Scotland 55 57N 4 40W	
30 Port Harcourt, Nigeria 4 40N 7 10E	
26 Port Hedland, Australia 20 25S 118 35E	
7 Port Laoise, Ireland 53 2N 7 20W	
26 Port Lincoln, Australia 34 42S 135 52E	
27 Port Macquarie, Australia 31 25S 152 54E	
3 Port Moresby, Papua New Guinea 9 24S 147 8E	
39 Port of Spain, Trinidad 10 40N 61 20W	
27 Port Pirie, Australia 33 10S 137 58E	
31 Port Said = Bûr Saîd 31 28N 32 6E	
31 Port Sudan = Bûr Sûdân 31 28N 32 6E	
7 Port Talbot, Wales 51 35N 3 48W	
34 Portage la Prairie, Canada 49 58N 98 18W	
36 Portland, U.S.A. 45 35N 122 40W	
7 Portland Bill, Ft., England 50 31N 2 27W	
13 Pôrto, Portugal 41 8N 8 40W	
42 Pôrto Alegre, Brazil 30 5S 51 3W	
8 Portree, Scotland 57 25N 6 11W	
7 Portsmouth, England 50 48N 1 6W	
37 Portsmouth, U.S.A. 36 50N 76 20W	
13 Portugal, Rep., Europe 40 0N 7 0W	
42 Posadas, Argentina 37 47N 5 11W	
40 Potosi, Bolivia 19 38S 65 50W	
10 Potsdam, Germany 52 23N 13 4E	
7 Powys, Co., Wales 53 30N 3 30W	
11 Poznan, Poland 52 25N 16 55E	
10 Praha (Prague) Cz. 50 5N 14 22E	
14 Prato, Italy 43 53N 11 5E	
6 Preston, England 53 46N 2 42W	
8 Prestwick, Scotland 55 30N 4 38W	
33 Pretoria, S. Africa 25 44S 28 12E	
34 Prince Albert, Canada 53 15N 105 50W	
35 Prince Edward I., Canada 46 20N 63 0W	
34 Prince George, Canada 53 50N 122 50W	
34 Prince Rupert, Canada 54 20N 130 20W	
18 Prokopyevsk, 54 0N 87 3E	
6 Prome, Burma 18 49N 95 13E	
37 Providence, U.S.A. 41 41N 71 15W	
34 Prudhoe Bay, Australia 21 30S 149 30W	
18 Pskov, U.S.S.R. 57 50N 28 25E	
38 Puebla, Mexico 19 0N 98 10W	
38 Pueblo, U.S.A. 38 20N 104 40W	
42 Puerto Montt, Chile 41 22S 72 40W	
39 Puerto Plata, Dominican Rep. 19 40N 70 45W	
39 Puerto Rico I., W. Indies 18 10N 66 30W	
15 Pula, Yugoslavia 44 54N 13 57E	
42 Punakha, Bhutan 27 42N 89 52E	
42 Punta Arenas, Chile 53 0S 71 0W	
39 Puntarenas, Costa Rica 10 0N 84 50W	
40 Purus, R., Brazil 5 25S 64 0W	
25 Pusan, S. Korea 35 5N 129 0E	
25 Pyongyang, N. Korea 39 0N 125 30E	
13 Pyrénées, Mts., Europe 42 45N 1 0E	

Q

21 Qatar, st., Asia 25 30N 51 15E	
31 Qena, Egypt 26 10N 32 43E	
35 Quebec, Canada 46 52N 71 13W	
34 Queen Charlotte Is., Canada 53 10N 132 0W	
2 Queen Elizabeth I., Canada 75 0N 95 0W	
33 Quelimane, Mozambique 17 53S 36 58E	
38 Querétaro, Mexico 20 40N 100 23W	
22 Quetta, Pakistan 30 15N 66 55E	
22 Quezon City, Phil. 14 50N 121 0E	
12 Quimper, France 48 0N 4 9W	
40 Quito, Ecuador 0 15S 78 35W	

R

30 Rabat, Morocco 33 9N 6 53W	
3 Rabaul, Papua New Guinea 4 24S 152 18E	
14 Ragusa, Italy 36 56N 14 42E	
22 Rajkot, India 22 15N 70 56E	

37 Raleigh, U.S.A. 35 46N 78 38W	
17 Randers, Denmark 56 29N 10 1E	
22 Rangoon, Burma 16 45N 96 20E	
28 Rarotonga, I., Pacific Oc. 21 30S 160 0W	
21 Rasht, Iran 37 20N 49 40E	
9 Rathlin I., N. Ireland 55 18N 6 14W	
16 Rauma, Finland 61 10N 21 30E	
41 Ravenna, Italy 44 28N 12 15E	
22 Rawalpindi, Pakistan 33 38N 73 8E	
7 Reading, England 51 27N 0 57W	
41 Recife, Brazil 8 0S 35 0W	
34 Red Dear, Canada 52 20N 113 50W	
21 Red Sea, Africa/Asia 25 0N 36 0E	
10 Regensburg, W. Germany 49 1N 12 7E	
14 Réggio, Italy 38 7N 15 38E	
34 Regina, Canada 50 30N 104 35W	
12 Reims, France 49 15N 4 0E	
8 Reindeer L., Canada 57 20N 102 20W	
12 Rennes, France 48 7N 1 41W	
36 Reno, U.S.A. 39 30N 119 50W	
42 Resistencia, Argentina 27 30N 59 0W	
29 Réunion, I., Indian Oc. 22 0S 56 0E	
34 Revelstoke, Canada 51 0N 118 0W	
16 Reykjavik, Iceland 64 10N 22 0W	
15 Rhodes = Ródhos, I.	
10 Rhine, R., W. Germany 51 42N 6 20E	
* 33 Rhodesia, st., Africa 19 0S 29 0E	
7 Rhondda, Wales 51 40N 3 30W	
12 Rhône, R., France 43 28N 4 42E	
8 Rhum, I., Scotland 57 0N 6 20W	
41 Ribeirvo Prêto, Brazil 21 10S 47 50W	
28 Riccarton, N.Z. 43 32S 172 37E	
36 Richland, U.S.A. 46 15N 119 15W	
37 Richmond, U.S.A. 37 33N 77 27W	
18 Riga, U.S.S.R. 56 58N 24 12E	
15 Rijeka, Yugoslavia 45 20N 14 21E	
14 Rímini, Italy 44 3N 12 33E	
35 Rimouski, Canada 48 27N 68 30W	
41 Rio de Janeiro, Brazil 22 50S 43 0W	
42 Rio Gallegos, Arg. 51 45S 69 20W	
42 Rio Grande, Brazil 32 0S 52 20W	
36 Rio Grande, R., U.S.A. 35 45N 106 20W	
35 Riviére du Loup, Canada 47 50N 69 30W	
21 Riyadh, see Ar Riyal 24 40N 46 50E	
37 Roanoke, U.S.A. 37 19N 79 55W	
6 Rochdale, England 53 36N 2 10W	
12 Rochefort, France 45 56N 0 57W	
37 Rochester, U.S.A. 43 10N 77 40W	
27 Rockhampton, Australia 23 22S 150 32E	
37 Rockford, U.S.A. 42 20N 89 0W	
36 Rocky Mts., N. America 48 0N 113 0W	
15 Ródhos, I., Greece 36 15N 28 10E	
27 Roma, Australia 26 32S 148 49E	
14 Roma, (Rome) Italy 41 54N 12 30E	
42 Rosario, Argentina 33 0S 60 50W	
9 Roscommon & Co., Ireland 53 38N 8 11W	
17 Roskilde, Denmark 55 38N 12 3E	
2 Ross Dependency, Antarctica 70 0S 170 5W	
3 Ross Sea, Antarctica 74 0S 178 0E	
9 Rosslare, Ireland 52 17N 6 23W	
10 Rostock, E. Germany 54 4N 12 9E	
18 Rostov, U.S.S.R., 47 15N 39 45E	
8 Rosyth, Scotland 56 2N 3 26W	
8 Rotherham, England 53 26N 1 21W	
8 Rothesay, Scotland 55 50N 5 3W	
28 Rotorua, N.Z. 38 9S 176 16E	
10 Rotterdam, Neth. 51 55N 4 30E	
12 Roubaix, France 50 40N 3 10E	
12 Rouen, France 49 27N 1 4E	
35 Rouyn, Canada 48 20N 79 0W	
16 Rovaniemi, Finland 66 29N 25 41E	
18 Rovno, U.S.S.R. 50 40N 26 10E	
21 Rub'al Khali, desert, Saudi Arabia 21 0N 51 0E	
18 Rubtsovsk, U.S.S.R. 51 30N 80 50E	
7 Rugby, England 52 23N 1 16W	
11 Rumania, st. Europe 46 0N 25 0E	
15 Ruse, Bulgaria 43 48N 25 59E	
8 Rutherglen, Scotland 55 50N 4 11W	
32 Rwanda, st., Africa 2 30S 30 0E	
18 Ryazan, U.S.S.R. 54 40N 39 40E	
18 Rybinsk, U.S.S.R. 58 5N 38 50E	

S

10 Saarbrücken, W. Germany 49 15N 6 58E	
13 Sabadel, Spain 41 28N 2 7E	
23 Sabah, Malaysia 6 0N 117 0E	
35 Sable, C., Canada 43 29N 65 38W	
36 Sacremento, U.S.A. 38 39N 121 30E	
37 Saginaw, U.S.A. 43 26N 83 55W	
31 Sahara, desert, Africa 23 0N 5 0W	
23 Saigon, see Phan Bho Ho Chi Minh, Vietnam 10 58N 106 40E	
7 St. Albans, England 51 44N 0 19W	
8 St. Andrews, Scotland 56 20N 2 48W	
7 St. Austell, England 50 20N 4 48W	
34 St. Boniface, Canada 49 50N 97 10W	
39 St. Christopher, I., W. Indies 17 20N 62 40W	
7 St. David's Hd., Wales 51 54N 5 16W	
12 St. Etienne, France 45 27N 4 22E	
5 St. George's Chan., Br. Isles 52 0N 6 0W	
29 St. Helena, I., Atlantic Oc. 15 55S 5 44W	
6 St. Helens, England 53 28N 2 43W	
35 St. Hyacinthe, Canada 45 40N 72 58W	
35 Saint John, Canada 45 20N 66 8W	
35 St. John's, Canada 47 33N 52 40W	
37 St. Joseph, U.S.A. 39 40N 94 50W	
8 St. Kilda, N.Z. 45 53S 170 31E	
35 St. Lawrence, G. of, Canada 48 25N 62 0W	
35 St. Lawrence, R., Canada 49 30N 66 0W	
30 St. Louis, Senegal 16 8N 16 27W	
37 St. Louis, U.S.A. 38 40N 90 20W	
39 St. Lucia, I., Windward Is., 14 0N 60 50W	
12 St. Malo, France 48 40 2 0W	

12 St. Nazaire, France 47 18N 2 11W	
37 St. Paul, U.S.A. 44 54N 93 5W	
37 St. Petersburg, U.S.A. 27 45N 82 40W	
35 St. Pierre et Miquelon, N. America 46 49N 56 15W	
12 St. Quentin, France 49 55N 3 20E	
39 St. Vincent, I., Windward Is., 13 10N 61 10W	
24 Sakai, Japan 34 35N 135 27E	
19 Sakhalin, I., U.S.S.R. 51 0N 143 0E	
42 Salado, R., Argentina 35 40S 58 10W	
13 Salamanca, Spain 40 57N 5 40W	
23 Salem, India 11 39N 78 12E	
14 Salerno, Italy 40 40N 14 44E	
7 Salisbury, England 51 4N 1 48W	
33 Salisbury, Rhodesia 17 50N 31 2E	
7 Salisbury Plain, England 51 13N 2 0W	
41 Salvador, Brazil 13 0S 38 30W	
38 Salvador, st., Central America 13 50N 89 0W	
36 Salt Lake City, U.S.A. 40 45N 112 0W	
42 Salta, Argentina 24 48S 65 30W	
38 Saltillo, Mexico 25 30N 100 57W	
10 Salzburg, Austria 47 48N 13 2E	
3 Samar, I., Philippines 12 0N 125 0E	
18 Samarkand, U.S.S.R. 39 40N 67 0E	
24 Samsun, Turkey 41 15N 36 15E	
36 San Angelo, U.S.A. 31 30N 100 30W	
38 San Antonio, U.S.A. 29 30N 98 30W	
40 San Cristóbal, Ven. 7 35N 72 24W	
36 San Diego, U.S.A. 32 50N 117 10W	
39 San Fernando, Trinidad 37 45N 122 30W	
36 San Francisco, U.S.A. 37 45N 122 30W	
39 San Francisco de Macoris, Dominican Rep. 19 19N 70 15W	
39 San José, Costa Rica 10 0N 84 2W	
36 San Jose, U.S.A. 37 10N 121 57W	
42 San Juan, Argentina 31 30S 68 30W	
39 San Juan, Puerto Rico 18 29N 66 6W	
40 San Luis Potosí, Mex. 22 10N 101 0W	
14 San Marino, Rep. Italy 43 56N 12 25E	
42 San Miguel de Tucumán, Argentina 26 47S 65 13W	
38 San Pedro de las Colonias, Mexico 25 50N 102 59W	
13 San Salvador, Salvador 13 40N 89 20W	
13 San Sebastian, Spain 43 17N 1 58W	
21 San'a, Yemen 15 27N 44 12E	
39 Sancti Spíritus, Cuba 21 52N 79 33W	
17 Sandviken, Sweden 60 38N 16 46E	
39 Santa Ana, Salvador 14 0N 89 40W	
36 Santa Ana, U.S.A. 33 48N 117 55W	
36 Santa Barbara, U.S.A. 34 25N 119 40W	
36 Santa Barbara Is., U.S.A. 33 40N 119 40W	
39 Santa Clara, Cuba 22 20N 80 0W	
39 Santa Cruz, Tenerife 28 29N 16 26W	
42 Santa Fé, Argentina 31 35S 60 41W	
40 Santa Marta, Colombia 11 15N 74 13W	
13 Santander, Spain 43 27N 3 51W	
41 Santarém, Brazil 2 25S 54 42W	
13 Santarém, Portugal 39 12N 8 42W	
42 Santiago, Chile 33 24S 70 50W	
39 Santiago, Dominican Rep. 19 30N 70 40W	
13 Santiago, Spain 42 52N 8 37W	
39 Santiago de Cuba, Cuba 20 0N 75 49W	
42 Santiago del Estero, Argentina 27 50S 64 20W	
39 Sar.to Domingo, Dominican Rep. 18 30N 69 58W	
42 Santos, Brazil 24 0S 46 20W	
42 São Carlos, Brazil 22 0S 47 50W	
41 São Luís, Brazil 2 39S 44 15W	
41 São Marcos, B. de, Brazil 2 0S 44 0W	
42 Sao Paulo, Brazil 23 40S 46 50W	
42 São Roque, C. de, Brazil 5 30S 35 10W	
12 Saône, R., France 46 25N 4 50E	
24 Sapporo, Japan 43 0N 141 15E	
15 Sarajevo, Yugoslavia 43 52N 18 26E	
18 Saransk, U.S.S.R. 54 10N 45 10E	
18 Saratov, U.S.S.R. 51 30N 46 2E	
23 Sarawak, Malaysia 2 0N 113 0E	
14 Sardinia, I., Italy 40 0N 9 0E	
17 Sarpsborg, Norway 59 16N 11 12E	
24 Sasebo, Japan 33 15N 129 50E	
34 Saskatoon, Canada 52 10N 106 45W	
14 Sássari, Italy 40 44N 8 33E	
21 Saudi Arabia, st., Asia 26 0N 44 0E	
35 Saulte Ste. Marie, Canada 46 30N 84 20W	
37 Savannah, U.S.A. 32 4N 81 4W	
14 Savona, Italy 44 19N 8 29E	
6 Sca Fell, Pk., England 54 27N 3 14W	
6 Scarborough, England 54 17N 0 24W	
7 Scilly, Is., England 49 55N 6 15W	
8 Scotland, U.K. 57 0N 4 0W	
37 Scranton, U.S.A. 41 22N 75 41W	
6 Scunthorpe, England 53 35N 0 38W	
36 Seattle, U.S.A. 47 36N 122 20W	
12 Seine, R., France 49 28N 0 15E	
18 Semipalatinsk, U.S.S.R. 50 30N 80 10E	
24 Sendai, Japan 38 15N 140 50E	
30 Senegal, R., Senegal 16 30N 15 30W	
30 Senegal, st., W. Africa 14 30N 14 30W	
35 Sept Iles, Canada 50 13 66 22W	
18 Serov, U.S.S.R. 59 40N 60 20E	
33 Serowe, Botswana 22 18S 26 58E	
12 Sète, France 43 25N 3 42E	
18 Sevastopol, U.S.S.R. 44 35N 33 30E	
6 Severn, R., U.K. 52 15N 2 13W	
18 Severodinsk, U.S.S.R. 64 27N 39 58E	
13 Sevilla, Spain 37 23N 5 58W	
34 Seward, Alaska 60 0N 149 30W	
29 Seychelles, Is., Indian Oc. 5 0S 56 0E	
31 Sfax, Tunisia 34 49N 10 40E	
10 s'Gravenhage, Neth. 52 7N 4 17E	
18 Shakhty, U.S.S.R. 47 0N 40 10E	
25 Shanghai, China 31 15N 121 30E	
9 Shannon, R., Ireland 53 10N 8 10W	
25 Shantou, China 23 25S 116 40E	
6 Sheffield, England 53 23N 1 28W	
27 Shellharbour, Australia 34 31S 150 51E	

* Renamed Zimbabwe